FUNDAMENTALISM
in
American Religion
1880 - 1950

A forty-five-volume facsimile series
reproducing often extremely rare material
documenting the development of one of the
major religious movements of our time

■ *Edited by*
Joel A. Carpenter
Billy Graham Center, Wheaton College
■ *Advisory Editors*
Donald W. Dayton,
Northern Baptist Theological Seminary
George M. Marsden,
Duke University
Mark A. Noll,
Wheaton College
Grant Wacker,
University of North Carolina

A GARLAND SERIES

■ Modernism
and Foreign Missions
Two Fundamentalist Protests

Edited with an introduction by
Joel A. Carpenter

Garland Publishing, Inc.
New York & London 1988

For a list of the titles in this series, see the final pages of this volume.
The facsimile of *Modernism in China* has been made from a copy in
the Billy Graham Center of Wheaton College, that of
Modernism and the Board of Foreign Missions has been made from a
copy in the Moody Bible Institute.

Library of Congress Cataloging-in-Publication Data

Modernism and foreign missions : two fundamentalist protests / edited
by Joel A. Carpenter.
    p. cm. — (Fundamentalism in American religion, 1880-1950)
Reprint.
First work originally published in Princeton theological review, 1921.
Contents: Modernism in China /W.H. Griffith Thomas — Modernism
and the Board of Foreign Missions of the Presbyterian Church in the
U.S.A. / J. Gresham Machen.
    ISBN 0-8240-5025-8 (alk. paper)
    1. Modernist-fundamentalist controversy. 2. Missionaries—China
3. Thomas, W.H. Griffith (William Henry Griffith), 1861-1924.
4. Presbyterian Church in the U.S.A. Board of Foreign Missions.
I. Carpenter, Joel A. II. Thomas, W.H. Griffith (William Henry
Griffith), 1861-1924. Modernism in China. 1988. III. Machen, J.
Gresham (John Gresham), 1881-1937. Modernism and the Board of
Foreign Missions of the Presbyterian Church in the U.S.A. 1988.
IV. Series.
BT78.M7 1988
273'.9—dc19

        88-5919

Design by Valerie Mergentime
Printed on acid-free, 250-year-life paper
Manufactured in the United States of America

CONTENTS

INTRODUCTION

This volume makes available two of the most influential documents of the fundamentalist protest against the spread of liberal theology and social gospel ministries within the Protestant missionary enterprise. The fundamentalist-modernist controversies of the 1920s and early 1930s may be remembered most often as a fight over "domestic" issues, such as the degree of doctrinal latitude that denominations ought to allow, or whether evolutionary theories had a rightful place in the nation's schools. But one of the most explosive issues was in fact related to Protestant churches' "foreign policy," their overseas missions. Fundamentalists mobilized on the mission fields as well as in the United States, and their allies on the home front made the question of what their denominations' foreign missionaries ought to believe and do central to their campaign to defend the "faith once delivered to the saints."

The role of missions in the controversies should come as no surprise, because the missionary enterprise was a central concern of the major North American Protestant denominations. The Northern Baptist Convention offers a particularly telling example. The various societies among northern Baptists were organized into a national denomination in 1907, with the consolidation of Baptist support for world evangelization as its major stated purpose. By 1921, the Northern Baptist Convention's missionary program involved over 800 missionaries and 7,000 native workers, who served in 1,800 churches, 4 colleges, 2,700 schools, 24 hospitals, and 62 dispensaries scattered over ten different fields. The Convention gave over $1.3 million (roughly 14 percent of its unified national budget) to support this work.[1] The Northern Baptists, of course, represented only one prominent effort in the collective North American Protestant missionary enterprise, which had reached staggering dimensions by the 1920s. According to one account, Americans and Canadians supported some 15,000 Protestant foreign missionaries with a total of over $48.6 million in 1922. This amounted to nearly 70 percent of the total missions income and over half of the total number of missionaries for Protestants worldwide.[2]

This massive commitment to overseas missions was shared by theological liberals and conservatives alike. Indeed, the Protestant missionary enterprise enjoyed a remarkable consensus concerning its primary beliefs, aims, and tasks during its heyday from 1890 to 1920. The statement of purpose published in 1920 by the Board of Foreign Missions of the northern Presbyterian denomination fairly represents that shared mission, which was

> to make Jesus Christ known to all men as their
> Divine Saviour and Lord and to persuade them to become
> his disciples; to gather these disciples into Christian
> churches which shall be self-propagating, self-supporting,
> and self-governing; to cooperate, so long as necessary,
> with these churches in the evangelizing of their
> countrymen and in bringing to bear on all
> human life the spirit and principles of Christ.[3]

The growing differences between liberals and conservatives regarding the nature of Christ's divinity, the inspiration and authority of the Bible, the Church's social mission, or the relative worth of other religions had not prevented them from working together to achieve their common desire to "make Christ known" and to make new disciples worldwide.[4]

This consensus was not to last, however, and the documents presented herein show it in the process of being shredded. As early as 1910, a report from China prepared for the World Missionary Conference held that year in Edinburgh noted that some sparks were flying between missionaries who held differing views of the Bible's inspiration and authority.[5] Tensions in North America quickly crossed the ocean as new volunteers—who had learned liberal theology and social gospel perspectives in northern universities, colleges, and seminaries—encountered old hands and Bible-school-trained recruits who were conservatives. This confrontation was probably the sharpest in China, where American missionaries were heavily engaged in higher education and in social-service endeavors such as the YMCA. Liberal perspectives prevailed in these agencies, but conservative evangelicals also had their strongholds, particularly among the missionaries representing southern denominational boards and in the largest missionary society in China, the China Inland Mission. This independent, international agency was militantly evangelistic and theologically conservative.[6]

Theological tensions grew in the context of a larger crisis. China's republican revolution of 1911 had aroused fervent nationalistic and anti-imperialistic protest movements, especially among students, and missionaries were close at hand to receive the brunt of these protests. Due to the anti-foreign violence and growing demands that the missionaries leave in the 1920s, the whole missionary enterprise in China was at risk. Doubts about its effectiveness and its integrity began to surface in American public discourse, in the sending churches, and even among some of the missionaries.[7]

Theological liberals and conservatives interpreted the situation in fundamentally different ways and tended to accuse each other of exacerbating the problems. Liberals saw the crisis as the birth pangs of a new democratic order in China. In this dynamic situation, liberals argued, the static dogmas of the conservative missionaries would be rejected and Christianity's future in China would be imperiled as a result. The task of liberals, then, was to prove themselves worthy allies in the struggle for democracy and modernization. By encouraging their students' critical search for truth and justice, they would prove Christianity's friendship to the "New Thought Movement" then sweeping through China's educated classes.[8]

Conservatives, on the other hand, feared the effect on the Chinese of the liberals' near-equation of social service with evangelism and their propagation of critical views—on the Bible's authority, traditional Christian doctines, and Christianity's exclusive claims. These perspectives, conservatives warned, would convince the Chinese nationalists that Christianity was either not true or a non-universal, disposable set of western ideals. They cited instances of Chinese students becoming agnostics under the influence of liberal missionaries' teaching. The best answer to China's turmoil, conservatives insisted, was to preach a simple, unadorned gospel, stripped of any attachment to programs of westernization and democratization. In the summer of 1920, conservative missionaries moved to counter the growing liberal Protestant influence. They formed the Bible Union of China to rally their forces, propagate their position, and lobby mission boards to carefully screen candidates for doctrinal orthodoxy. Within two years, some 2,000 missionaries—about 30 percent of the total missionary force—were members.[9]

The conservative protest against modernism in China played a critical role in heating up the fundamentalist-modernist controversy in the United States, especially in the northern Presbyterian denomination. Indeed, historian William Hutchison credits W. H. Griffith Thomas, author of the first document in this book, "Modernism in China," with "firing the first shot" in the ensuing fight.[10] The other document published herein, *Modernism and The Board of Foreign Missions of the Presbyterian Church in the U.S.A.*, by J. Gresham Machen,[11] might well be called the "last offensive" of the militant conservatives to counter liberalism in that denomination. Indeed, one illuminating way of understanding the course of the fundamentalist-modernist controversy among northern Presbyterians is to follow the chain of events leading from "Modernism in China" to *Modernism and the Board of Foreign Missions.*

The story behind Thomas's article, "Modernism in China," is instructive because it links the anti-modernist movement in China to the fundamentalist movement in North America. William Henry Griffith Thomas (1861–1924) was an Anglican seminary professor who served at Wycliffe Hall, Oxford, from 1905 to 1910, and then at Wycliffe College of the University of Toronto from 1910 to 1919. He was a popular author and speaker in the dispensationalist, "higher Christian life," and Bible school network that formed the core of the emerging fundamentalist movement. Thomas resigned his position at Wycliffe College in 1919 to devote full time to writing and conference speaking, and he was a featured speaker at the conference in Philadelphia that same year, which launched the World's Christian Fundamentals Association.[12]

Thomas traveled to Japan and China in the summer of 1920 with Charles G. Trumbull, who was editor of the influential fundamentalist weekly, the *Sunday School Times,* and chief organizer, teacher, and promoter of the Victorious Christian Life Council, an organization which sponsored speakers and conferences on personal holiness and spiritually effective living, after the fashion taught by British evangelicals at the famous conferences in Keswick, England. According to Trumbull, this trip to the Orient was occasioned by invitations from missionaries and Chinese Christians to hold "Victorious Life" conferences at various spots in China, and particularly at several summer resort conferences frequented by missionaries.[13]

One invitation in particular made the trip financially possible, though; it was from J. H. Blackstone, a missionary in China and the on-site agent for the Milton Stewart Evangelistic Fund. This foundation supported the work of conservative evangelical missionaries, conference speakers, native evangelists, and Bible schools in China. It was funded by one of the principal stockholders of the Union Oil Company, whose brother, Lyman Stewart, had been the chief financial backer of *The Fundamentals,* the twelve-volume conservative publication series (1910–1915) that launched the public career of fundamentalism.[14] So, while both Thomas and Trumbull claimed that they did not go to China to stir up a controversy, they were already involved in fundamentalist campaigns in the United States and much of their funding came from a pro-fundamentalist foundation. Indeed, Thomas seems to have been advised before his visit that since he was sure to stir up controversy, he should not speak on controversial topics, but to let his audience initiate them.[14]

Nevertheless, when Thomas arrived at the large missionary resort at Kuling, in central China, he spoke to fundamentalist issues: "The Authority of the Bible, Inspiration, Old Testament Criticism, Evolution, The Place and Power of Scholarship, and The Lord's Coming." Thomas spoke for a second conference week, this time with some lively give-and-take before an audience of both liberals and conservatives. Soon after Thomas and

Trumbull departed, their conservative hosts formed the Bible Union of China, with an initial membership of four hundred, and a leadership committee of thirty—half of whom, according to one account, were affiliated with the China Inland Mission or the Southern Presbyterian Mission.[16]

As Thomas and Trumbull spoke elsewhere in China, they saw or heard about plenty of instances of liberal theology and social-gospel dampened enthusiasm for evangelism. On January 24, 1921, Thomas addressed the Presbyterian Social Union in Philadelphia on the subject of modernism in China. The substance of his remarks appeared in the *Sunday School Times* that April,[17] and in "Modernism in China," the article reprinted herein, which appeared in the *Princeton Theological Review* in October.

"Modernism in China" is more about the growing alarm of conservative missionaries in China and their efforts to oppose modernism through the formation of the Bible Union than it is about modernism and its adherents. Although Thomas cites some concrete evidence of liberal theological texts being used and commended, and of liberal perspectives in some articles and addresses by prominent American and Chinese church leaders, the greater part of this article is a justification of the Bible Union and an answer to those who criticized its divisiveness.

Thomas's point was that modernism was a major force among China missions, and that it was a mistake to blame him for bearing bad tidings or accuse him of being an agitator. Wherever he went in China, he reported, distinguished conservative missionary leaders informed him of the pervasiveness of liberal theological perspectives, the erosion of active evangelism in the face of increased efforts in education and social service, and the anxiety and confusion of many Chinese Christians as they confronted these developments. People at home should be aware of these facts and they should know that conservative missionaries were justified in mobilizing against modernism. The article ends with a plea for mission boards to carefully examine missionary candidates on their views of the Bible's authority and other fundamental doctrines; and if they cannot recall modernists from the field, then they should "prevent any more such from going out" (pp. 669–70).

Thomas's address provoked an immediate response from the conservative forces in the northern Presbyterian Church. The conservative journals were fulminating over this issue in the spring of 1921, and by the time of the General Assembly that summer, five presbyteries submitted overtures requesting that the Board of Foreign Missions be instructed to appoint only doctrinally orthodox missionaries. Thanks to the skillful defense of Robert E. Speer, the distinguished missionary statesman who was Secretary of the Board, the Standing Committee on Foreign Missions reported to the General Assembly that the Board of Foreign Missions and its missionaries were trustworthy. The Assembly did instruct the Board to examine the reports of modernism on the mission field; but since no specific charges were submitted, the Board reported that the accusations were groundless. Militant conservatives' complaints continued sporadically but the Board faced no more serious challenges during the 1920s.[18]

One of the most important reasons why the Board of Foreign Missions was able to breathe easier for a while was that the "domestic" side of the fundamentalist-modernist controversy was heating up. But what is not often recognized is that the tensions in China prompted a curious sequence of events which actually drew attention away from the missions arena. Harry Emerson Fosdick, a liberal Baptist professor of homiletics at Union Theological Seminary and the stated preacher at the First Presbyterian Church of New York, was invited to spend the summer of 1921 on the conference circuit in China. His sponsors, the Federal Council of Churches, the YMCA, and Standard Oil magnate John D. Rockefeller, Jr., hoped that Fosdick could pour some oil, as it were, on the waters that had been troubled the previous summer by the fundamentalists. Fosdick was rather successful, but he came home convinced that the fundamentalists constituted a very real danger to the liberal movement and to the tolerant spirit of mainstream Protestantism.[19]

On May 21, 1922, Fosdick delivered a sermon which grew out of this experience, "Shall The Fundamentalists Win?", which blasted away at the "immeasurable folly" of one party trying to drive others out of the churches because of differing theories publicist and distributed widely, precipitated the full-blown fundamentalist-modernist conflict in the northern Presbyterian Church.[20] Issues, people, and institutions that were much closer to home than China came to the fore in these debates, such as Fosdick's standing in the Presbyterian Church, the Auburn Affirmation (a manifesto for theological inclusiveness signed by 1,294 Presbyterian clergy), the militantly conservative J. Gresham Machen's nomination to a chair of apologetics at Princeton Seminary, and the reorganization of Princeton Seminary to make it more theologically inclusive.[21] As a result, fundamentalists' attention was diverted away from the mission fields.

These events prepared a charged setting, however, in which the "modernism and missions" issue could explode once more, given a spark. And the repeated defeats of the militant conservatives and their champion, Professor J. Gresham Machen, often at the hands of the moderate conservatives who controlled the Board of Foreign Missions, pointed to yet another showdown.

Machen (1881–1937) was a brilliant New Testament scholar and apologist whose works, *The Origin of Paul's Religion* (1921), *Christianity and Liberalism* (1923), *What Is Faith?* (1925), and *The Virgin Birth of Christ* (1930), earned him esteem as a scholar and great notoriety as a conservative defender of the faith. He had a devoted following among the students at Princeton, and was the chief controversialist for the militant conservatives in his denomination. Since he was not one to practice the arts of patience, compromise, and support-winning which a movement's leadership demands, things did not go well for him or his followers.[22]

Indeed, by the early 1930s, the party of doctrinal precisionists and ecclesiastical exclusivists which Machen led had become increasingly alienated from the centers of influence in the northern Presbyterian Church. They had lost the battle over whether their strict interpretation of the church's historic creeds or the "Auburn Affirmationists'" doctrinal toleration should prevail. Machen suffered further humiliation and defeat when his nomination for the chair of apologetics and ethics at Princeton Seminary was debated on the floor of the 1926 General Assembly and sent back to Princeton for reconsideration. And the 1929 General Assembly confirmed a plan to reorganize the Seminary in order to open it to alternatives to the militant Calvinist conservatism which prevailed there. In that same year, Machen and three other professors left Princeton to establish Westminster Theological Seminary in Philadelphia.[23]

Machen and his followers were losing hope for restoring a doctrinally conservative church. They had found, to their extreme frustration, that their most powerful opposition came from moderate conservatives such as Charles Erdman at Princeton Seminary and Robert Speer at the Board of Foreign Missions. Machen was especially embittered by the leadership these two gave to the reorganization of Princeton Seminary. These moderates, Machen concluded, were papering over theological differences for the sake of denominational peace and prosperity, and were misleading the public as to the dangerous situation in the Church's agencies. Because of their unwillingness to stand for the truth and expose error, and because they covered up the extent to which modernism had pervaded the denomination, Machen insisted that they, not the liberals, had become the most dangerous enemies to the orthodox cause.[24]

With Westminster Seminary and *Christianity Today*, a semimonthly magazine founded in 1930, the militants rallying around Machen had a stronghold from which to cultivate their movement, disseminate anti-modernist and anti-moderate propaganda, and let events take their course. Some hoped for a gradual reform of the denomination through the influence of Westminster graduates, but Machen was prepared to leave the denomination should another showdown come. According to a recent biographer, Machen was waiting for an opportunity to force the issue once again and to rally conservative support for a new departure.[25]

His opportunity came in 1932, with the publication of *Re-Thinking Missions,* a one-volume version of the seven-volume report of the Laymen's Inquiry on Missions, a project initiated in 1930 and funded by John D. Rockefeller, Jr. This Inquiry also had the informal encouragement of seven denominational missions boards. The Inquiry commissioned the Institute for Social and Religious Research (another Rockefeller project) to survey mission work in India, China, Japan, and Burma; and it also sent a Commission of Appraisal to tour the mission areas. Much of the Inquiry's Report focused on practical suggestions, such as improving overseas social work, upgrading the professional quality of missionaries, and turning over the churches to indigenous leadership.

The far more disturbing aspect of the Report, especially as articulated in *Re-Thinking Missions,* was the religious re-thinking that the chief contributor of the theological section, William E. Hocking, was urging. Hocking, a philosopher at Harvard, called for missions to depart from a conversionist agenda and to enlist other religions in a partnership of "world faith" that would counter the relentless sweep of secularity. Hocking's views were a radical departure from the earlier liberal-evangelical missions consensus, that had insisted on the superiority, finality, and indispensability of Christianity. *Re-Thinking Missions* incensed American Protestant conservatives, and mission board leaders seemed deeply embarassed by it. In an atmosphere already charged by fundamentalist-modernist friction, any praise for the Report would alienate conservatives, and too stern a condemnation would anger liberals. The official responses thus tended to be rather tepid, and they pleased no one.[26]

That was precisely the situation in the northern Presbyterian Church. Robert Speer, secretary of the denomination's Board of Foreign Missions, wrote what one historian called a "polite rebuttal" to the Report, in which he praised its practical suggestions, but criticized W. E. Hocking's questioning of Christianity's exclusivity and finality and his obvious distaste for evangelism.[27] Predictably, Professor Machen was not satisfied with such even-handed treatment of a document which he considered to be an outright attack on historic Christianity. The bland demurrals of Speer and the Board of Foreign Missions rankled him; what was needed was a trumpet blast against such apostasy. After nearly a decade of voicing complaints and suspicions regarding the Board's attitude toward theological liberalism, Machen was convinced that he now had the evidence he needed to press the issue in the church tribunals.[28]

Just as Machen was building his case, Pearl Buck, a Presbyterian missionary to China whose novel *The Good Earth* (1931) won the 1932 Pulitzer Prize, inadvertently highlighted his argument. In a well-publicized public lecture and in two articles in prominent magazines, Buck praised *Re-Thinking Missions* lavishly and underscored its critiques of the missionary enterprise. The Board of Foreign Missions, not wishing to make Buck a martyr, soft-pedalled the issue throughout the spring of 1933. Buck offered to resign in late April, and the board accepted, expressing "deep regret." But by this time, Machen was embroiled in a bitter fight over the Foreign Board. The Board's silence on such a blatant expression of religious modernism was the last straw for him.[29]

On January 24, 1933, Machen presented an overture to the Presbytery of New Brunswick, which urged the General Assembly to instruct the Board of Foreign Missions to: (1) elect to the Board only those who adhere to the fundamentals of the Christian faith (biblical infallibility, and Christ's virgin birth, miracles, substitutionary atonement, and bodily resurrection); (2) to instruct the Board that no one who will not insist on subscription of these doctrines by every missionary candidate can be Candidate Secretary; (3) to instruct the Board to see that faithfulness to the gospel and opposition to false doctrine are conveyed as norms in all its blanks and forms and dealings with candidates; and (4) to warn the Board about the danger of union enterprises in light of widespread doctrinal error.[30] The Presbytery put this overture on the docket for its April 11, 1933 meeting, and with Machen's permission, invited Robert Speer to be present to respond to this overture.[31]

Machen then drew up his arguments and documentation for this meeting, which is the second piece in this book: *Modernism and the Board of Foreign Missions of the Presbyterian Church in the U.S.A.* [32] This 110-page pamphlet discusses and presents evidence for six major grievances against the operation of the Board: (1) its lack of outrage over *Re-Thinking Missions*; (2) its soft-pedalling of the Pearl Buck case; (3) its sympathy to the Auburn Affirmation; (4) the Candidate Department's endorsement of "modernist propaganda"; (5) a theologically inclusivist bias in the Board's candidate reference and application forms; and (6) the Board's theologically indiscriminate interdenominational cooperative policies. Most of these complaints seem, in hindsight, to be tiresome and ungracious nit-picking. And yet they show how incensed Machen was at the Board's theological vagueness, its unwillingness to make distinctions between theological truth and error, and the apparent pro-modernist stance of several of its officers.

A seventh grievance, which is presented in the final forty-five pages of the text, seems much more serious; it concerns the existence of modernism in enterprises supported by the Board in China. This section consists of lengthy communiques from Dr. Albert B. Dodd, a Presbyterian missionary professor in the North China Theological Seminary, and from Chancellor Arie Kok of the Netherlands Legation in Peiping. These pieces, which are replete with transcribed addresses, reprinted articles, and like documentation, present the sort of name-naming, incident-and-substance citations for which Griffith Thomas's "Modernism in China" and Machen himself in an earlier skirmish were criticized for not providing. These documents present rather convincing evidence that at least a few Presbyterian missionaries and Presbyterian-supported ventures in China were propagating theologically liberal and politically radical perspectives. It is rather curious, then, that Machen makes no summation to conclude this section. It gives every appearance of having been "tacked on" at the last moment to add gravity to Machen's earlier charges and arguments.

Machen's major point of attack, then, was the Board's doctrinal pacifism and "indifferentism." He was convinced that the Christian church was engaged in a battle of epic proportions, in which his modernist adversaries were firing such salvos as *Re-Thinking Missions*. But avowedly orthodox leaders like Speer would not take to the firing line on these issues. Speer, to Machen, represented a reprehensible "'middle-of-the-road' tendency" in the conflict between biblical orthodoxy and modern doctrinal indifferentism (p. 59). Nothing seemed to anger and frustrate Machen more than what he called "this palliative or reassuring attitude which, we are almost inclined to think, constitutes the most serious menace to the life of the Church today; it is in some ways doing more harm than clear-sighted Modernism can do" (p. 60).

On April 11, Machen presented a summary of these grievances and his evidence for them before the Presbytery of New Brunswick. Robert Speer declined to answer them point-for-point, but simply argued that the overture was improper and unconstitutional, and that the vast majority of Presbyterian missionaries were truly evangelical. He closed with an appeal for peace and unity. Machen's overture was defeated by a voice vote, and then a resolution was passed commending Speer and the Board.[33] Machen was deeply disappointed, especially because Speer made no answer to the charges.[34] But thanks to the publicity of *Christianity Today* and *The Sunday School Times,* Machen sent out thousands of copies of *Modernism and the Board of Foreign Missions* to inquirers. Machen would get further chances to argue his case, since the Philadelphia Presbytery endorsed the overture the following month. But again the winsome presence of the great missionary statesman Speer brought overwhelming defeat, this time at the General Assembly in late May.[35]

Machen and his followers repudiated the Board, and in effect, the denomination. What followed was their bitter retreat to the outback of American religious life. They formed the Independent Board of Presbyterian Foreign Missions later in the summer of 1933, and defied a ruling at the next General Assembly that such activity was illegal for church office-holders. Over the next two years, Machen and many of his followers were tried and suspended from the ministry. In 1936, Machen and a faithful remnant of his once-substantial conservative following founded what became known as the Orthodox Presbyterian Church. Machen struggled doggedly on to organize a viable denomination, but died of pneumonia on January 1, 1937, while campaigning for his church in the Dakotas.[36]

Speer retired that same year, weary of conflict, but with his Board intact. His retirement, suggests historian James Patterson, marked the end of an era. The primary significance of the conflicts over the goals and substance of the missionary enterprise, however, was not the defeat of the fundamentalists. Indeed, the protests of Griffith Thomas and J. G. Machen functioned as declarations of conservative evangelicals' independence from the old-line Protestant missionary enterprise. In the ensuing years, while the old-line denominational missions have declined, the ones sponsored by fundamentalists and other evangelical groups have grown steadily. By 1980, evangelical boards accounted for over 90 percent of the 35,000 career missionaries from North America.[37] But this development had some hidden costs, evangelicals discovered. In the long run, perhaps the most important outcome of the conflicts over modernism in missions has been the destruction of the consensus that Protestant missionary enterprise once enjoyed. And the loss of that consensus has been felt most keenly in the field of missions theory. Even while conservative evangelical missions are thriving, some of the movement's leaders are just now discovering the issues of Christianity and culture that confronted the missions establishment some sixty years ago. Because of their separation, the heirs of fundamentalism are being forced to reinvent the whole discussion.[38]

Joel A. Carpenter
Institute for the Study of American Evangelicals
Wheaton College

NOTES

1. Robert G. Torbet, *Venture of Faith: The Story of the American Baptist Foreign Mission Society and the Woman's American Baptist Foreign Mission Society, 1814–1954* (Philadelphia: Judson Press, 1955), 175–77, 411–14.

2. Harlan P. Beach and Charles H. Fahs, eds., *World Missionary Atlas* (New York: Institute of Social and Religious Research, 1925), 69 (income), 76 (total Protestant missionaries), 82–97 (total North American missionaries).

3. Robert E. Speer, *Are Foreign Missions Done For?* (New York: Board of Foreign Missions of the Presbyterian Church in the U.S.A., 1928), 56.

4. Two works that give helpful summaries of this missionary consensus are James A. Patterson, "The Loss of a Protestant Missionary Consensus: Foreign Missions and the Fundamentalist-Modernist Conflict," in *Earthen Vessels: American Evangelicals and Foreign Missions, 1880–1980*, ed. Joel A. Carpenter and Wilbert R. Shenk (Grand Rapids: Eerdmans, 1989), forth coming; and William R. Hutchison, "Modernism and Missions: The Liberal Search for an Exportable Christianity, 1875–1935," in *The Missionary Ent erprise in China and America*, ed. John K. Fairbank (Cambridge, Massachu setts: Harvard University Press, 1974), 126–31.

5. M. Searle Bates, "The Theology of American Missionaries in China, 1900–1950," *Missionary Enterprise in China,* 151.

6. Paul Hutchinson, "The Conservative Reaction in China," *Journal of Reli gion* 2 (July 1922): 340–43, 347–50; Paul A. Varg, *Missionaries,Chinese, and Diplomats: The American Protestant Missionary Movement in China, 1890–1952* (Princeton: Princeton University Press, 1958), 212–17.

7. *Ibid.,* chapter IX, "The Crusade Runs into Stumbling Blocks at Home Base, 1919–1931," 147–66; Varg, "The Missionary Response to the Nationalist Revolution," 311–35, and Shirley Stone Garrett, "Why They Stayed: American Church Politics and Chinese Nationalism in the Twenties," 283–310, both in *Missionary Enterprise in China.*

8. A classic statement of this position is in Hutchinson, "The Conservative Reaction in China," 338–39, 355–61.

9. Bates, "Theology of American Missionaries," 150–54; W. H. Griffith Tho mas, "Modernism in China," *Princeton Theological Review* 19 (October 1921): 630–71; Hutchinson, "Conservative Reaction," 343–47.

10. Hutchison, *Errand to the World: American Protestant Thought and Foreign Missions* (Chicago: University of Chicago Press, 1987), 139.

11. Machen, *Modernism and the Board of Foreign Missions of the Presbyterian Church in the U.S.A.* (Philadelphia: by the author, 1933).

12. Helpful information on Thomas's career is in the first chapter of Rudolf A. Renfer, "A History of Dallas Theological Seminary" (Ph.D. dissertation, University of Texas, 1959). Thomas was an important participant in a plan

to develop a fundamentalist seminary, although he did not live to see the Evangelical Theological College (later, Dallas T. S.) founded in 1926.

13. Trumbull, "Victorious Life Conferences in the Far East," *Sunday School Times,* May 1, 1920, 245–46. For an introduction to (and critique of) the Keswick "Higher Christian Life" movement and Charles G. Trumbull, see Douglas W. Frank, *Less than Conquerors: How Evangelicals Entered the Twentieth Century* (Grand Rapids: Eerdmans, 1986), 109–23, 145–54.

14. This incident nicely illustrates the connections within the early fundamentalist network. Blackstone's father, William E. Blackstone—who was the author of the vastly popular and influential millenarian treatise, *Jesus Is Coming* (1st ed., 1878)—administered this fund for Milton Stewart. This incident is discussed in Trumbull, "Victorious Life Conferences," 245–46; and Ernest R. Sandeen, *The Roots of Fundamentalism: British and American Millenarianism, 1800–1930* (Chicago: University of Chicago Press, 1970), 249–50. George Marsden discusses the Stewarts' respective projects in Marsden, "Introduction," *The Fundamentals: A Testimony to the Truth,* 12 original volumes reproduced and bound as 4 volumes, vol. 1 (New York: Garland Publishing, 1988); and Joel Carpenter outlines W. E. Blackstone's career in Carpenter, "Introduction," *The Premillennial Second Coming: Two Early Champions* (New York: Garland Publishing, 1988).

15. Thomas, "Modernism in China," 630.

16. Hutchinson, "Conservative Reaction," 343; Thomas, "Modernism in China," 630–36.

17. Thomas, "Missions in China: Their Strength and Weakness," *Sunday School Times,* April 16, 1921, 211–12; April 23, 1921, 224–25.

18. A good account of this episode is in James Alan Patterson, "Robert E. Speer and the Crisis of the American Protestant Missionary Movement, 1920–1937" (Ph.D dissertation, Princeton Theological Seminary, 1980), 130–37. Further citations will show that the rest of my introduction owes more to this excellent dissertation than to any other scholarly source.

19. Robert Moats Miller, *Harry Emerson Fosdick: Preacher, Pastor, Prophet* (New York: Oxford University Press, 1985), 105–09.

20. *Ibid.,* 112–117; Patterson, "Robert E. Speer," 129; George M. Marsden, *Fundamentalism and American Culture: The Shaping of Twentieth-Century Evangelicalism, 1870–1925* (New York: Oxford University Press), 171–73. For a full text of Fosdick's sermon, see *The Fundamentalist-Modernist Conflict: Opposing Views on Three Major Issues,* ed. Joel A. Carpenter (New York: Garland Publishing, 1988).

21. Edwin H. Rian, *The Presbyterian Conflict* (Grand Rapids: Eerdmans, 1940) is a thorough, though partisan (fundamentalist) account of these debates; as is Lefferts A. Loetscher, *The Broadening Church* (Philadelphia: Westminster Press, 1957), from the moderate/liberal perspective. Marsden also summarizes these events in *Fundamentalism,* 173–77, 180–81, 183–84, 192.

22. Biographical studies of Machen include Ned B. Stonehouse, *J. Gresham Machen: A Biographical Memoir* (Grand Rapids: Eerdmans, 1954), by one of Machen's disciples; C. Allyn Russell, "J. Gresham Machen, Scholarly Fundamentalist," in Russell, *Voices of American Fundamentalism: Seven Biographical Studies* (Philadelphia: Westminster Press, 1976), 134–61; and Darryl Hart, "*Doctor Fundamentalis:* An Intellectual Biography of J. Gresham Machen" (Ph.D dissertation, The Johns Hopkins University, 1988).

23. Russell, "J. Gresham Machen," 150–56; Stonehouse, *J. Gresham Machen,* 351–93; 408–68.

24. *Ibid.,* 372–76, 389, 471–72; Patterson, "Robert E. Speer," 138–44.

25. Hart, "*Doctor Fundamentalis,*" chapter 8, ms., 18–19.

26. Hutchison, *Errand to the World,* 164–65; Patterson, "Speer," 95–98.

27. Hutchison, *Errand,* 169 (quote)–171; Patterson, "Speer," 98–114.

28. Hart, "*Doctor Fundamentalis,*" ch. 8, ms., 19–22.

29. Hutchison, *Errand,* 166–69; Patterson, "Speer," 145–47, 152–55; Machen, *Modernism and the Board of Foreign Missions,* 16–18.

30. Stonehouse, *Machen,* 475–76.

31. Machen, *Modernism,* 3.

32. According to James Patterson, *Modernism* is a much-expanded version of an unpublished paper that Machen sent Speer during an earlier exchange over missions issues in 1929. Patterson, "Speer," 149.

33. Machen, *Modernism*, 3; Patterson, "Speer," 150–51; Stonehouse, *Machen,* 478–80.

34. Speer would answer Machen's charges in detail in papers for the General Assembly's Standing Committee on Missions. Patterson, "Speer," 151–52.

35. Stonehouse, *Machen,* 480–81.

36. *Ibid.,* 482–508.

37. Patterson, "Speer," 190; Hutchison, *Errand,* 176–77.

38. For more fulsome discussions of this point, see "Familiar Debates in an Unfamiliar World," the last chapter of Hutchison, *Errand* (176–202); Grant Wacker, "Liberal Protestant Perceptions of World Religions and the Search for a Missions Mandate, 1890–1940"; and Charles Van Engen, "Reluctant Pilgrims: Developments in Evangelical Theology of Mission, 1943–1984," both in *Earthen Vessels: American Evangelicals and Foreign Missions, 1880–1980,* forthcoming.

MODERNISM IN CHINA

As this article is a narrative of some experiences of a recent visit to China, it is necessarily concerned with personal matters, and I am compelled to use the first person in order to state how certain questions arose, so far as I was concerned. Before leaving America I was advised by one who knows the Chinese situation not to introduce controversial topics in any of my addresses but to leave these to be mentioned by missionaries, which, it was said, was certain to be the case. I gladly endorsed and carefully observed this suggestion, but, finding myself (due to railroad difficulties) at the well-known holiday resort of Kuling for a week more than had been originally planned, I was requested by missionaries who favoured the conservative view of things to give a series of six lectures. I agreed to do so on the distinct understanding that they were to be quite separate from the official Convention fixed for the following week, and that they were to be announced as intended only for those who wished to hear these subjects discussed. By request I submitted four topics, which were accepted, and I was asked to add to these any two others which I thought would be useful. The result was that I spoke on, The Authority of the Bible, Inspiration, Old Testament Criticism, Evolution, The Place and Power of Scholarship, and The Lord's Coming. The last-named was one of the four accepted subjects.

I prefaced my first lecture with certain statements which I felt would help to make the situation clear. I said that I had been invited to give the lectures, and had been left practically free to choose my subjects; further, that it was thoroughly understood these addresses were no part of the Convention which was to follow, and that only those who wished to hear them were expected to attend. I added that there was no desire merely to antagonize other views, but only to say frankly and fairly what conservatives held on these subjects.

Then, further, during the ordinary Convention in the following week, I took, by the request of several workers, the general subject of "Grounds of Christian Certainty," and dealt with six of these: The Person of Christ, The Death of Christ, The Resurrection of Christ, The Bible, The Church, and Christian Experience.

I soon found to be true what I had learned long before I left America, that missionaries were already divided into two camps, those who favoured critical views and those who were strongly conservative. One result of my lectures during the first week was to bring out these differences more acutely, and both opposition and approval were abundantly manifest. In the course of the Convention I was asked to conduct (according to the custom of former years) a Question Box, and having had occasion to use Dr. Driver's treatment of the Flood story as a proof in my judgment of the impossibility of accepting the current critical dissection of the narrative, the following question came from a Professor in a Theological Seminary:

You ridiculed Dr. Driver's analysis of a verse in the Flood record. Do you deny the composite character of the Flood narratives? If so, how do you account for the fact that the two documents, J and P, give a fairly complete narrative, and that these narratives do not harmonize?

To this I replied that I had no intention of ridiculing Dr. Driver, but only of showing from one verse the characteristics of his entire treatment, which, in my opinion, was unthinkable. I then pointed out that the two documents, J and P, do not give a "fairly complete narrative," because P omits several important details which are supplied in the intervening J sections, and J is so fragmentary as not to deserve being called an account, for it needs for completeness the very matters that P contains. The result is that criticism is compelled to call in the assistance of R, an editor, a circumstance which, however interesting, does not make the theory any more convincing. As to the documents not harmonizing, I urged that there is only a lack of harmony when the narrative is divided, and I called special attention to one great fact which Professor Sayce maintains is crucial, namely, that the Babylonian account of the Flood, written ages before the date assigned by criticism to J and P, contains sections strikingly like the J and P documents.

Another question was sent in by the same writer, and I cannot do better than give this in full:

> Why labour so hard to drive a wedge of distrust between two great bodies of Christian workers whose loyalty to Christ is undoubted, by attempts to show that there is no room for the supernatural in any view except the extremely conservative one which you represent? How can we work together if the conservatives think there is no room for the supernatural in the position held by the liberals?"

I replied that I was not driving a wedge between two bodies of workers, for a wedge was already there, and I said that I had been told of this before I left America. Further that since my arrival in China, I had received ample proof of the fact of this division, and I proceeded to give some facts from missionaries. These will be incorporated later in this paper. I also repelled quite definitely the idea that I had in any way suggested there was no room for the supernatural in the position held by the Liberals. What I had said, and what I still maintain, is that the inevitable tendency of Liberalism on the Bible is to minimize the supernatural, and that the logical outcome is Rationalism. I also called attention to the statement of Dr. Orr, that it is impossible to fit orthodox conclusions into a Wellhausen framework. As to the two bodies of missionaries working together, I said that this was obviously a question to be settled by the missionaries themselves. On this point I never expressed an opinion. I also urged the importance of taking care lest Liberalism should be intolerant, because as long as conservatives are silent there is an outward appearance of unity, but when they begin to speak out on behalf of their own position, they are said to be causing division, though, in reality, the cause of division is the introduction of the new views.

At the end of one of the meetings, a missionary came to me and said that he wished to give me one illustration of the fact that the trouble was far earlier than the present time and had existed for several years. In his station, a Chinese Christian magazine had been regularly taken and put into the reading-room. At first it was edited by a well-known Methodist missionary and subsequently by an equally well-known Canadian Presbyterian. When the latter had to leave China for his furlough, the work of editing was undertaken by a missionary of another Church, one of the best-known men in China. I purposely avoid naming him or his church though the missionary who told me the story gave me full details. Not long after the new editor had been at work, one of the Chinese helpers of the missionary who mentioned the matter to me went to him and asked that the magazine might be discontinued. As the missionary had not had time to read it himself, he naturally asked the reason of this request. The Chinese worker said that there was a series of articles written by the editor on the subject of Buddhism, wherein statements were made about Buddhism which he (the Chinese helper) did not want the converts to see.

At the close of my series of addresses, a resolution was passed at Kuling, and I hope it is not too personal to insert here. I only do so in order to show what missionaries of the conservative type feel on these topics:

Whereas Dr. Thomas, actuated by a deep interest in the progress of Christ's Kingdom in China and in missionaries of all denominations has kindly come from America to address us and our Chinese co-workers and has worked energetically and unremittingly in giving the excellent course of addresses which it has been our privilege to hear; and whereas it is proper that we give some expression to the gratitude we feel for the valuable service he has rendered, and to our appreciation of the high qualities of a Christian minister which Dr. Thomas has exhibited in his work. Therefore we note with warm commendation his high scholarship, wide reading and careful and accurate investigation of the subjects discussed, the interesting manner in which these subjects were treated; his earnestness and deep spirituality; his fairness in dealing with those who differ; his courteous and conciliatory spirit, combined with courage and candour;

above all his profound devotion to the Lord Jesus Christ, to the Holy Scriptures and to the great Fundamental Truths of the Gospel. We acknowledge with gratitude the great benefit we have received from these addresses and from personal contact with the man, and express our hearty thanks for this "labour of love"; and we wish Dr. Thomas Godspeed in the work to which he returns in America, and shall follow him with grateful remembrance and with our prayers.

Passed by a rising vote of the whole congregation on behalf of the Kuling Community, July 1920.

This was accompanied by the following letter of thanks from Dr. Henry M. Woods of the Southern Presbyterian Mission, who is, as is well known, a leading missionary and scholar:

My dear Dr. Thomas:

I take pleasure in sending herewith a copy of the resolutions passed by a rising vote by the Kuling Congregation this morning. Allow me to say that these resolutions are not a mere polite form but express, I believe, the sincere feelings of this community as a whole. Your work has met admirably a great want among the missionaries in China. It is, I believe, no exaggeration to say it is the most important work which can be done in China; for it lies at the root of all successful missionary work. If the missionaries are poisoned with doubt and are not true to God's Holy Word, what hope is there of leading the Chinese pastors and people to true faith? Do urge the friends at home *to continue this good work every year* and send out able, scholarly and spiritual men to give stirring addresses on the Fundamentals and point out the errors of so-called New Theology. God bless your work abundantly. You carry back the cordial esteem of all of us.

Sincerely,

(Signed) HENRY M. WOODS.

At this point it will be convenient to mention what happened at Kuling after I left. A new organization was formed called "The Bible Union of China," and as I have just received the first number of the *Bulletin* issued by the Union I cannot do better than give extracts from it to show what was being felt by missionaries and the action that was taken in the formation of the Bible Union. These are the opening words of the memorandum about the origin of the Union:

For several years there has been a growing concern in the minds of many missionaries of various denominations because of the teaching of destructive critical views of the Bible, which teaching has been gradually introduced into some mission centres in China. The conviction has been growing that those who accept the whole Bible as the revealed Word of God and emphasize the Atoning Sacrifice of Christ should unite their efforts in strengthening the position of the Christian fundamentals and protect the Chinese Church from those who would assail this position.

During the 1920 Kuling Convention it was discovered that without any previous conference or comparison of views several men of different missions and denominations were thinking and working along the same line, i.e., to formulate some common statement acceptable to all who stand for the Bible in its entirety, to which they could subscribe, thus banding themselves together in the interest of the conservation of sound doctrine.

The outcome of this was the publication of a tentative statement in preparation for a general meeting which was to be held last February:

Being convinced that the state of both the Christian and non-Christian world demands unity of purpose and steadfastness of effort in preaching and teaching the fundamental and saving truths revealed in the Bible, especially those now being assailed, such as, the Deity of our Lord and Saviour Jesus Christ, His Virgin Birth, His Atoning Sacrifice for Sin, and His Bodily Resurrection from the Dead; the Miracles both of the Old and New Testament; the Personality and Work of the Holy Spirit; the New Birth of the Individual and the necessity of this as an essential prerequisite to Christian Social Service:

We reaffirm our faith in the whole Bible as the inspired Word of God and the ultimate source of authority for Christian faith and practice;

And unitedly signify our purpose "to contend earnestly for the faith once for all delivered unto the saints."

To this end we express our desire to join with others of like mind in seeking to carry out the following Program:

1. Prayer: To pray that God may so direct this movement as to arouse the Church of Christ to its deep need of a firmer grasp on the fundamentals of the Christian faith and a fresh realization of the power and sufficiency of the simple Gospel of our Lord Jesus Christ, the preaching and teaching of which has been blessed of God since the beginning of Missionary work.

2. The Bible: To promote the circulation, reading and study of the Bible, trusting that its Divine Author will use this movement as a testimony to its integrity and authority.

3. Literature: To prepare and circulate literature and textbooks witnessing to the fundamental truths of the Bible.

4. Personnel: To present to our Home Boards and supporters the vital importance of accepting for missionary service only such candidates as accept the truths referred to above.

5. Educational Institutions: To stand firm for faithful teaching of the whole Bible as of primary importance in the work of all Christian Schools and Colleges; and also by deputation work, conferences and special lectureships, help forward local effort in emphasizing the fundamentals of the Christian faith.

6. Theological Education: To promote sound teaching in theological seminaries and Bible schools and to seek means by which able exponents of the faith may reach the present and future leaders of the Chinese Church.

7. Evangelism. To forward all measures in Christian enterprises which make for the deepening of their devotional, evangelistic, and missionary spirit.

To show the widespread feeling on these subjects it may be mentioned that up to December last the enrollment of members was just over 600, and I am told that since then there have been further and large accessions.[1] One of the editorial notes in the *Bulletin* is as follows:

From nearly every section of China as well as from the homeland of many of us letters have come expressing hearty appreciation of the Bible Union movement. Many see in it the answer to the prayers and heart longings of years. That this movement has been opposed, misunderstood, and in some cases misrepresented need not discourage anyone. If God be for us and this movement be of His ordering, as we most surely believe it is, then neither opposition nor misrepresentation will be able ultimately to hinder its work.

The committees appointed represent practically every society and no one can look at the names without realising that the Bible Union indicates and proves the seriousness of the situation as it is felt by a large body of Chinese missionaries.

Among the committees formed was one on Personnel, the object of which, as stated above, is "to present to our Home Boards and supporters the vital importance of accepting for missionary service only such candidates as accept the truths referred to above." The *Bulletin,* in noting that the work of this Committee is of such a nature as to be best accomplished after the membership roll is fairly complete and when a permanent committee is appointed, remarks that in the meantime "it is certainly proper for us as

---

[1] Up to September 1921, 1400.

members of the Bible Union to acquaint our home friends with the main purposes of the Bible Union and solicit their prayers that those candidates who are selected and sent out may come bearing only the Truth which makes men free."

It will be readily seen from these statements that I had nothing to do with the formation of the Bible Union, except in so far as my addresses seem to have been the immediate *occasion* for it. Certainly they were in no sense the *cause,* for the trouble was of long standing, and something would have been done in any case, sooner or later. And yet this is what the editor of *The Continent* allowed himself to say in March last: "The organization of the new Bible Union of China is another bit of mischief for which Dr. Griffith Thomas is responsible, along with his travelling companion, Mr. Trumbull, the editor of The Sunday School Times." I wonder how the hundreds of missionaries of various churches will feel at seeing the Bible Union being described as a "bit of mischief"! If the matter were not so serious it would be ludicrous to read another statement which appeared in this article in *The Continent,* that "before these travellers went to China, both sorts were working together in brotherly love and common loyalty to Christ." There are missionaries of long standing who could tell a very different story.

In *The Moody Bible Institute Monthly* for September, 1921, a letter appears from the Secretary of the Bible Union, the Rev. W. R. Williams of Luho. This is part of what he says of the Union:

Your sympathetic interest in the Bible Union of China was to be expected. The need for this united movement had become imperative. Dr. W. H. Griffith Thomas and Mr. Charles G. Trumbull found out some of the conditions here, but not all. Thank God, they are making effective use of what they got.

If the church at home is aroused by the facts which they give, their visit will have been a thousand times worth while. It is high time that supporters of missionaries in all foreign lands realize that the missionary can do no other than beget children, spiritual children, "in his own likeness, after his image," just as did Adam.

You may like to pass on to your readers information as to the Bible Union of China.

It is just about 1,250 now, and still growing daily.

This membership is made up of persons connected with more than eighty different denominations or missionary societies. At least the following nationalities are represented: English, Scotch, Irish, Norwegian, Swedish, Finnish, German, Russian, Danish, Dutch, Canadian, American and Australian.

After leaving Kuling, I visited several other places, and my experiences must be briefly narrated. At Peitaiho, another summer resort for missionaries, I had the great privilege of speaking twice or three times each day for about ten days, and although they were workers of different theological views, and opportunities were given for frank discussion, there was no difficulty, still less opposition, encountered. But not far from Peitaiho was another "colony" of missionaries, most of whom desired me to give a series of addresses to them. This request met with strong opposition from several workers, chiefly connected with the Y. M. C. A., who thought that my coming would "divide the missionaries." But the wishes of the majority prevailed, and I gave five addresses.

When I went to Peking, I learned of the existence of what is known as the Peking Apologetic Group, a number of Christian men whose aim is to confer with Christian and non-Christian leaders on Christian subjects and social problems. This group issues a monthly magazine known as *Life*, and in an editorial some months ago, the purpose and contents of the magazine were stated. Christian theology was said to be "truly a mysterious and very difficult problem," and the assertion was made that, "because of the misinterpretations of Christian theology," many regard Christianity as unworthy of attention. The magazine also expressed its intention to interpret theological questions "according to the latest scientific methods, and criticise and correct any errors of interpretation therein." This is, of course, an eminently praiseworthy object in itself, though everything depends on the meaning attached to the terms used and the way in which the work is done.

In Shanghai, I heard still more of the inroads of Higher Criticism, and three of the most impressive testimonies came from Dr. Walter Lowrie of the Presbyterian Church, U. S. A.; Mr. D. E. Hoste, Director of the China Inland Mission; and Mr. Rankin, a lawyer connected with the Southern Methodist University of Soochow. Dr. Lowrie spoke very strongly at a public meeting against Modernism, and said that Evangelicals had been silent for a long time in the hope of improvement being seen, but this attitude had become an impossible one; and now there are two schools of missionaries, the fundamental difference between them being whether or not the Bible can be trusted. He added that for many years past he had seen a weakening in the preaching of the New Testament Christ. Further, that the Arians of the fourth century did not dare to say to Athanasius that the New Testament was unreliable; this was left to be said in the twentieth century. Dr. Lowrie also said that to substitute anything for salvation from sin was to proclaim "another Gospel," and this should be so declared to the infant Church of China. He remarked that the term "Modernism" was a euphonious description of ancient Arianism and Latitudinarianism. Mr. Hoste said that it was unnecessary to talk of dividing the missionaries, because they were already divided, and that while he had sympathy with all possible forms of coöperation in missionary work, he was conscious that beneath the coöperation there was a fundamental difference as to the message. Mr. Rankin has been out in China for eight years, and he said that he had no idea until he arrived there as to the extent of the Higher Critical peril. He had come to the conclusion that it was essential for laymen of his Church to know precisely what was being done with their money, and he had, therefore, taken steps to acquaint them with the facts. As I listened to the calm, quiet statement of this lawyer, I could not help feeling impressed with its evident reality. It seemed to me to do far more than prove anything that I had noticed during my brief visit to China.

When I reached Canton, I was soon made aware of similar conditions in that city. The two parties were as much in evidence as in other places, and although there was no outward and visible indication of severance, one missionary said to me that while there was plenty of coöperation in Canton, there was no real union of heart. After my return home, I read an article in an English magazine entitled "Modernism in China," written by a Methodist clergyman, the Rev. Henry E. Anderson, who is at present working as a representative of the British and Foreign Bible Society. I wish it were possible to reproduce the entire article, which is full of impressive statements. The writer opens by remarking that "it is increasingly evident that the cleavage between those who hold the conservative views of theology and those who are termed Modernists is becoming more and more pronounced every day," and that "even those who occupy a neutral position will soon be forced to declare themselves for one side or the other." This cleavage is then said to be becoming very marked on the mission field, and that it is very tragic that Christian workers should have their simple faith undermined. One missionary who holds a chair in a theological seminary told Mr. Anderson that he had only one fault to find with Higher Critics, that they did not go far enough, and at this college it is reported that the question was recently discussed with all seriousness as to whether it would be advisable to drop all instruction from the Old Testament, since some thought that these books were of no more value than the Confucian classics. This is how Mr. Anderson states the position in Canton:

In the great city of Canton for example there is not a single missionary out of about two hundred who have their headquarters there, set apart for purely evangelistic work in the city itself. All the missionaries are engaged in institutional work of one kind or another or are occupied with country work, and it is supposed that the Chinese workers are undertaking the task of evangelizing this great city of nearly two million population. The work is not being done as it should be done, and it will never be done at all, if it is left to these supposedly highly-trained men who are shaky in their theological convictions, and who hold loose views about the authority and inspiration of the Bible.[2]

Facts such as these, which can be adduced from other places as well, led to serious consideration of the place given to education, and it was hardly possible for me to avoid the question whether, in some missions, undue emphasis was not being placed on education in contrast with evangelism. I know, of course, that very many workers are doing magnificent service in evangelization, and nothing I now say is intended for an instant to detract from their fine and self-denying work. But side by side with this I could not help feeling that, in several centres and missions, evangelism was being set aside by purely secular educational work. I am well aware that with the huge illiteracy in China educational work is essential, but there is a serious risk of its being regarded as an end instead of a means, and also of its being separated from the evangelism which is the supreme task of the Church.

In this connection, Dr. Bowen, President of the University of Nanking, has some significant remarks in his latest *Annual Report*:

While Christianity is distinctively a mystical and a spiritual religion it is nevertheless extremely and supremely practical for the "man in the street," and herein lies another great problem that missionary education in general and our University in particular needs to study. How often have we been disappointed when some student or graduate has been placed in a definite situation and has neither had the spirit nor ability to cope with it in anything resembling a masterful manner. We have felt again and again that at some point or points our education was lacking in applying the spirit of the Christianity and the truth that we teach to the actual world in which the student lives. What we tell him in school never reaches his plane of living. His thinking and doing are entirely separated by what is often apparently a blank wall. In some way this wall must be broken through, and our school work must be made to minister to the actual necessities of life.

---

[2] *Journal of the Wesley Bible Union*, London, England, February, 1921.

In view of the clear recognition of this problem by so prominent a worker in China, it is not unsuitable that I should call attention to it. There is no danger at all if education and evangelism are kept constantly together, because to educate one who has been evangelized is to provide the best possible equipment for the service of God. But to educate without evangelizing is to involve the Chinese in serious moral peril. To show that I am not dealing with imaginary dangers, let me quote from one who is engaged in educational work and is also a keen soul-winner: "To see these lads going out from us after four years of the best training we can give them in science and agriculture and arts, and yet without that which of all we can give is the most important, is heartbreaking."

Dr. Robert Fitch of Hangchow, who is himself engaged in educational work, raised the question in *The Chinese Recorder* for August, 1920, as to how it is that, while in educational and medical missions every precaution is taken to get the best quality of teachers, evangelism is almost allowed to take care of itself. It would be of great service to reproduce a material part of Dr. Fitch's article, which appeared to me to prove beyond question the serious risk to which I am now calling attention.

Another instance of the peril can be seen in some words spoken by Dr. Luella Miner before the Chihli-Shansi Educational Association a year or so ago:

We hope that many will remain in our church work, evangelistic, educational, medical and industrial, and that those who go into occupations not directly connected with the churches will as voluntary workers take a large share in the church life as leaders in Sunday-school, prayer meeting, personal work, Christian Associations and many lines of social service. Yet our present educational system provides no definite training for such service. In fact, the hours of credit allowed in our Middle Schools and Colleges for the department of Biblical History and Literature and Religious Education are not sufficient for even a smattering of knowledge. In the curriculum for Middle Schools prepared for this Association, out of thirty-six semester hours of work, only one is given to this department, less than is allowed in many secular schools in America. There, sixteen units are required for graduation from the four years' High School course, a unit being approximately one-fourth of a full year's work, or 120 hours of class room work. Where they have twenty hours a week, we have thirty-six hours. North Dakota and Indiana allow one-half unit for their department of Biblical and Religious Education and Iowa one unit. Even at the lowest rate of one-half unit, the proportion is one to thirty-two, while ours is one to thirty-six, and this with no government restrictions to hinder our giving this department full working efficiency.

Passing to colleges, even some tax-supported colleges in the United States allow more credits for this department than we provide in our Christian Universities; for example, the State University of North Dakota out of 120 semester hours allows thirty-two hours in Biblical History and Literature and Religious Education to count toward a degree.

Suppose that a graduate of a Higher Primary School planned after leaving Middle School to go into business, or industrial work, or a girl into home life or church work, do we in our present Middle School course, provide them with the electives which would enable them to fit themselves to be efficient lay workers in the church? If we did, there would be less distress when leaders are sought for "follow up work" in connection with meetings like those held under the leadership of Dr. Eddy and Miss Paxson. Even our college graduates now need special training classes to equip them for work in our Sunday-schools and Bible Sunday groups.

No type of missionary is more needed in each educational center in China than the one who can correlate the work in mission schools and churches, and link all more closely with community life. And in our entire educational system we should keep in mind the need of trained lay workers in the church, and of teachers for the department of Biblical History and Literature and Religious Education in schools of all grades. Middle Schools should train teachers for Primary School, Colleges for the Middle School, and the Graduate School or Senior College should train the specialist, the educator, the man capable of research work. This is outside the ordinary theological college curriculum. If we develop truly fine departments of religious education in our Mission Universities, and our graduates in character, in capacity and devotion to community service of various forms commend themselves to the nation, is it too much to hope that the time may come when students in government schools may take a certain proportion of semester hours in Christian Middle Schools, Colleges, or Universities, and receive full credit therefor in the government schools? Our aim should not be less than this, for so only can we render the greatest service to China. In science and mathematics we can hardly hope to surpass, in equipment or quality of teaching, the government schools. Our distinct contribution may be in the moral and spiritual realm, where we must recognize educational values equally high.[3]

It is evident from these words that the problem of religious education in relation to evangelism is a grave one in China, and calls for immediate and thorough attention by those who believe in the New Testament teaching about the purpose for which Christians are sent into the world. It is not merely theoretical to remark that it is imperative beyond all else to "keep first things first."

Another problem in China is that of the "returned student," the man who has been to America and obtained a degree there. He often returns home to China with views of the Bible and Christianity which are definitely critical. The result is, as may be expected, that his teaching and influence are all against the true New Testament Gospel of Christ. One of these who is on the staff of a Christian institution and possesses an American degree was lecturing not long ago to a class of young men, and told them that all nations have certain national stories, which are not true, but are told for the moral value of the incidents. Thus, he said, every American mother tells her children the story of Washington and the Cherry Tree, which, though not true, is told for its influence in connection with truthfulness. Then the speaker added that the story of the Resurrection of Christ is not true, but is told for its moral bearing on the doctrine of immortality. This statement greatly perturbed a young, earnest, inquiring Chinese, and it was only with the greatest difficulty that the error was corrected and the truth set before him.

This is only one illustration out of several that could be given, showing the seriousness of the situation in connection with student life. Reference has already been made to the monthly magazine for students published in Peking, entitled *Life*. In a recent issue of this magazine there was an article on "The Problem of the Creed" by Professor T. C. Chao, who is on the staff of a Christian university and

[3] Quoted in the *Annual Report* of the China Sunday School Union.

is regarded as one of the ablest and most brilliant of the young Chinese scholars who have obtained their degrees in America. Professor Chao, according to *The Chinese Recorder* for November last, began by apologizing for writing upon so important a subject as the Apostles' Creed and for offering a presentation of his own. He gave ten reasons for his hesitation to make known his ideas. But he said that he could not keep these truths to himself, and felt compelled to share his views with others and to tell what had been fermenting in his mind during the last half-year. The criticism of the Apostles' Creed is summed up in five points:

(1) The Creed, he thinks, contains in some statements mere historical facts which cannot be considered real articles of faith; inasmuch as such statements—the crucifixion, death, and burial of Jesus—may be scientifically ascertained or rejected; (2) the Creed contains certain unessential elements which debar many serious-minded persons from confessing Christ openly; (3) the Creed does not contain anything of a Christian view of society—the Kingdom of God is not mentioned at all though it forms a very essential part of Jesus' teaching; (4) the Creed dwells on things merely physical and metaphysical, and not moral, containing no statement about any ethical standard or any moral demand on man; it is therefore very unsatisfactory and out of harmony with the spirit of our modern thought and life; (5) finally the Apostles' Creed does not say a thing about the character of Jesus Christ who is the center of the Christian religion.

After thus criticising the Creed, Professor Chao goes on to say that this statement of the Christian faith was due to the necessity of the times in which it appeared, and that as our day is so very different from earlier times, it is necessary to reconstruct the statements of our faith for the sake of the Christian religion as well as for the good of earnest people. Then the writer indicates ten requirements for a sound creed and, in accordance with these requirements, he formed a creed for his own use which is as follows:

1. I believe in God the Creator, Ruler, and Sustainer of the Universe and our holy loving father who is also our moral ideal.

2. I believe in Jesus who, through holy living and sacrificial love, achieved character and became God's Only Begotten Son, equal to God in essence, glory, and eternity and able to reveal God's nature and man's possibilities to us, thus having right to be our Teacher, Brother, Friend, and Saviour.

3. I believe in the Holy Spirit, the Spirit of God and of Christ, who seeks to save man and desires that men on account of his love forsake sin and be reconciled to Him, have fellowship and work together with Him in order that they may expand their spiritual life, realize their moral character, and acquire strength to glorify God and serve men.

4. I believe that whosoever has Christ's mind and shares his life and death, glory and shame, purpose and work, is a Christian; Christ has eternal life, so Christians also have eternal life.

5. I believe that Christians form a united Church through spiritual fellowship, using visible organizations such as denominations as instruments for the realization of the life and spirit of Christ in men.

6. I believe in the gradual realization of the kingdom of heaven, which is the realization of a new humanity and a good social order, and so I believe that, in the course of time, truth will become clearer to us, the Church will be purer, humanity will enjoy greater peace, and the world will possess a better civilization.

Now, to say nothing of the fact that these ideas have, on the writer's own admission, only been "fermenting in his mind" during half a year, while the Creed has obtained the loyal and convinced assent of some of the greatest minds of the Christian Church during centuries, what is to be said of the obvious crudeness, inadequacy, and inaccuracy of many of the views here set forth? The Professor has never faced such a book as Mozley's *Historic Christianity and the Apostles' Creed,* and it is clear that his own creed is wholly inadequate to the revelation of God in Christ found in the New Testament. There is evident need of someone taking this young man and "expounding to him the way of God more perfectly." Meanwhile serious injury is being done by the promulgation of such views as though they represented Christianity.

A few months ago a paper appeared in *The North China Daily News* on "Modern Radical Thought among Chinese Students" by the Rev. R. F. Lo and the Rev. Paul Hutchinson. It was a paper read at the winter meeting of the East China Educational Association and the original article extended to nearly six columns. The following extracts will indicate the present position:

So much for the non-Christian students. Presumably we all realize how the same currents are affecting the students who are under direct Christian influence. . . .

In an attempt to gauge this flow of radical thought we have obtained cross sections of classroom conversations from many of the leadings schools of East China, together with some discussions raised in summer conferences. It is impossible to give the results of this investigation as a whole. It is enough to say that we have not found a single student body in our schools not deeply affected by ideas which, whether in the realm of politics, economics, sociology or religion, can hardly be called orthodox. . . .

A study of these returns, however, leads to the opinion that in political, and certainly in social and economic matters, students are much more responsive to the suggestions of their teachers than in the realm of religion. Probably all teachers feel this, and for this reason we are just now experiencing something bordering on panic among certain teachers, and other Christian workers, who see their pupils launching out upon seas of religious discussion the farther shores of which are beyond our sight. It generally gives a hen who has hatched duck eggs a panic when her brood takes to the water, and a similar phenomenon is recognizable in some parts of the mission field today. . . .

It only remains to say that everywhere there is apparent a questioning by our students of the foundations of faith itself. The seed sown by radicals without our ranks is bearing fruit within. "Why should we have religion," a Christian student asks, "since it is superstition and causes stagnation in progress?" Christian worship is compared with the worship of idols by the ignorant, and all alike stigmatized as superstition. And in many and many schools there is evidence that thoughtful students, who have been under Christian instruction for years, are reaching the point where, over against all religion, Christianity as well as the rest, they are writing that sinister word: Superstition. . . .

Many of you who are here will recall echoes of these questions, or others even more startling, as you have heard them in your own classrooms, or in the sanctuary of your private talks with your pupils. You will know that we have not overdrawn the picture. We might have quoted many other questions, had they been needed to make our case. The case, we believe, is made. Within the schools conducted by the Christian church you will find as much radical thought, and thought as dangerous in its implications, as is to be found anywhere in this seething land. . . .

As proof that this rationalism is rife in China, reference may be made to the action of the East China Educational Association about a year ago. It recommended for inclusion in its curriculum of Bible study in middle schools,

two books from the Bible Study Union Lessons, and while
it is only fair to say that the recommendation was for the
pedagogical value alone and that the Association took no
responsibility for the doctrinal position of the writers, it is
surely wrong for a Christian educational association to
recommend, even on pedagogical grounds, to people who
have no religious knowledge of the various currents of
thought in the Western world, books which are so far removed from the plain teaching of Scripture. One of these
books is *The Life of Jesus*, by Forbush, and the following
extracts will show the character of the teaching:

Now we come to the explanation which the Gospels give of the
miracles. The class will readily see that they were all unscientific
and were thoroughly characteristic of the crude medical knowledge of
the time. . . . *We can never know just what Jesus did or how He did
it.* . . .

No matter how animated the discussion of miracles may be, close
the lesson hour with the practical point that our attitude to Him *does
not depend upon some external facts of two thousand years ago*, but
upon our allegiance to His living truth today.

It is easy to see that the age that produced the Gospels would not
be anxious for scientific accounts of the deeds of Jesus, but that it
would expect of Him exactly the acts that are attributed to Him. . . .

As nearly all the miracles not of healing had their prototypes in the
Old Testament, many of them at least *were attributed* to Jesus *because
men expected such deeds* from their Messiah and finally became convinced that He must have performed them. . . .

RE THE FEEDING OF THE MULTITUDES

If the class is curious to know exactly what happened beside the
lake the teacher's *honest answer* must be that *we can never know.*
The difficulties of this narrative are plain. We seek for honesty from
the evangelist, but we have no right to demand more. . . .

It is simply a question of evidence, and *the evidence is lacking.* . . .

RE THE HISTORICAL RESURRECTION

We want to fix attention *not upon a historical occurrence*, the records
of which are late and scanty, but upon the present experience of Christ
living in the disciple. . . .

That Jesus should have reappeared on earth, partly man and *partly
wraith*, and then disappeared again, does not give adequate proof to
us of the spiritual Jesus who helps us to live. . . .

We today tend to think that Jesus' resurrection was *not different
from our own*, that immediately the Father received the spirit, which

the dying Jesus committed unto Him, and that thenceforth He thus lives in the Father's keeping forever. . . .

While *it is impossible for us to be certain as to the details* of those experiences, since the written accounts appeared so many years after the death of Jesus, all Christians are united in certain great assurances.

In some of the details of the later Gospel accounts we recognize the answers which the early church was endeavoring to give to unbelievers in the resurrection who lived from thirty to fifty years after the crucifixion of Jesus. Those answers and explanations *are only incidental.*

Another book thus recommended is *The Story of the Bible,* by Hunting, and again the following extracts show the attitude of the author:

RE THE INSPIRATION OF THE BIBLE

In the preceding chapters we have had the story of the liberation of the Bible from the prisons of ecclesiastical tyranny, and of unknown tongues. In this chapter we have the story of its release from a *false theory of interpretation.*

After one has learned the exact meaning of any passage of the Bible, the next step is to form an *independent judgment regarding its essential truth* and moral value. An appeal must be made to one's own mind and conscience. . . . *Our own conscience is as truly the voice of God as is the Bible,* and its testimony must fearlessly be given a hearing.

Until recently it was considered quite wrong, if not blasphemous, to put the Bible to such a test. We were supposed to take for granted beforehand that whatever the Bible says is true. Yet only through this test can the Bible become to us, to the fullest extent, a source of inspiration. When we are forbidden to question whether or not a statement is true, we are prevented from appreciating *how* true it *really is.* When, on the other hand, we freely bring the Bible, and our own best instincts, face to face for mutual testing, it is as though an electric connection had been established between ourselves and the Bible message.

The old tendency to regard the Bible as an absolutely infallible book has been gradually modified in modern times through the development of science and a more careful study of the Bible itself.

In the nineteenth century, this kind of investigation grew to be an independent *science. . . .* This new science seems to show that the Bible is a very human book. The laws of Moses are now seen to be the product of centuries of experience on the part of the Hebrew people and were impressed on the minds and hearts of the Hebrew people *rather than written on tables of stone.*

It will probably be agreed that the second commandment, forbidding images, while no doubt a wise provision in those days, is not *in any way* binding today.

According to the Chronicler's representation of the matter the testimony of history was all on the side of the Jews. *Clearly* we *should not regard such a history as altogether reliable.* Not that the Chronicler deliberately falsified the history, but he lived in a *biased* atmosphere.

Re the Gospel of John

As Peake confesses, "The Johannine narrative is suspected to have been largely formed under the influence of definite theological preconceptions, or from the exigencies of theological controversy." . . .

This does not mean that the author of the Fourth Gospel deliberately distorted the history in the interests of theological doctrines, but only that he and his fellow-Christians at that time *were unconsciously influenced in their interpretation of the history by their theological beliefs.* . . .

John's description of the life of Christ may not be an absolutely perfect one. The nineteen centuries which have passed since John's time have doubtless taught us something; and *it seems to us in these modern days* that Jesus was more truly human than He appears in the great portrait of John. . . .

Was Jesus a mere man, or was he a superhuman being, with superhuman powers? Those who on general grounds have held the latter view have clung to the theory that the fourth gospel is the work of an eyewitness, because this gospel testifies so emphatically to certain superhuman elements in the personality of Jesus. Those, on the other hand, who on general grounds have believed that Jesus was a man like other men, to be classed with other great moral and religious leaders of history, have felt compelled to treat the fourth gospel as *the product of the idealizing imagination of a later age.* . . .

Many scholars find a growing tendency in early Christian literature, to define the divinity of Jesus not in these terms of moral uniqueness, but in terms of a metaphysical difference between the nature of Jesus and the nature of other men. *This really obscures the true moral supremacy of Jesus.* The picture of the Master in the Synoptic Gospels combines a marvelous human simplicity with a unique moral glory. Comparing this picture of Jesus with the picture in the fourth gospel, we seem to find in the latter a marked tendency to try to enhance the divinity of Jesus by obliterating his true humanity. On these general *a priori grounds,* therefore, it seems *difficult to regard the gospel as the work of an eyewitness.* . . .[4]

At this point it is necessary for me to deal with a somewhat personal matter, and my reason will be seen as we go on. It has been charged against Mr. Trumbull and me that

---

[4] These extracts were selected, and sentences printed in italics, by a member of the Committee in order to show to the rest of the Committee the type of Scripture interpretation used in two courses in this series.

we went to China at the expense of a Fund left "for the promotion of premillennial teaching," that we were there as "special pleaders, with a peculiar view of 'orthodoxy.' " On this I would say that there are several serious errors: (1) The Fund was not "left," but given, the donor being still alive. (2) It was not given "for the promotion of premillennial teaching," but for evangelistic work in China, and it includes in its help missions which are not premillennial. (3) Mr. Trumbull and I went out only in part "at the expense" of this Fund, a good share of the expense being met by the Victorious Life Council. (4) Neither Mr. Trumbull nor I was limited in any sense, expressed or implied, in regard to teaching. We were left perfectly free and without restrictions. (5) As a matter of fact, I spoke only about four times on the Lord's Coming out of something like two hundred addresses and sermons, and even these four were either by request or after approval, and two of them were in private drawing-rooms, at personal invitation, and followed by frank discussions. Not once did I take this subject solely on my own initiative and without consultation. From all this it will be seen how incorrect the charges are. I may add that during my time in China I met quite a number of missionaries who I knew were entirely opposed to my view of the Lord's Coming, and yet because we were heartily agreed on the authority and integrity of the Bible, we had the most delightful fellowship, and different views on the Second Advent had no effect whatever. These brethren are, of course, fundamentally different from those whose postmillenial views are based on Rationalism and denials of the plain statements of the Bible. In conversation with one well-known man who maintained that the real division was caused by the difference between premillennialism and postmillennialism, I asserted, what I now repeat, that the trouble is not due to any difference of views about the Lord's Coming but goes far deeper and is concerned with the authority of the Bible. In proof of this I wish to give one instance. In the number of *The Chinese Recorder* for August 1920, the following review occurs:

PREMILLENIALISM: NON-SCRIPTURAL, NON-HISTORIC, NON-SCIENTIFIC, NON-PHILOSOPHIC. *By* GEORGE PRESTON MAINS. *The Abingdon Press, New York, Gold $1.00 net.*

For those who are perplexed by this question or who desire a brief and untechnical discussion of it with which to offset the insistently promoted propagandist literature of its advocates, nothing will be more satisfactory than this book of 160 small pages. It is not as exhaustive as Dr. Snowden's scholarly *The Coming of the Lord*, nor as drastic as Dr. Shailer Matthews' *Will Christ Come Again?* It is clear, concise, convincing, and constructive. It can be especially recommended for English-speaking Chinese, and ought by all means to be translated.   J. L. S.

The initials of the reviewer are those of one of the best known and ablest missionaries in China. The book which he recommends in these warm terms is not merely a statement of the postmillennial view but is concerned with matters that are altogether opposed to the conservative view of the Bible. Thus, the author maintains that the premillennial idea grew out of Jewish apocalypticism dating from the second century, B. C., when, it is stated, Daniel was written. It is said that the Jews were so steeped in it that the Apostles could not shake it off, and, according to some of the writers quoted by the author, our Lord was likewise ensnared by this propaganda and led astray in His thinking. But the author goes on to say that two thousand years of history have exploded these ideas and rendered them untenable. The Apostles, including Paul, all laboured under the false ideas of their day, and their mistaken conceptions got into their teaching and into their epistles. In *The Christian Index*,[5] a Baptist paper published in Georgia, this book by Dr. Mains is reviewed, and after giving a number of proofs of its character, the writer ends with these words: "It is well for Evangelical Christians to realize that many scholars like Dr. Mains are doing untold injury to multitudes by destroying their faith in the Book with their claims to be historical, scientific and philosophical. How they can claim

---

[5] For July 1, 1920.

to be Scriptural is a mystery. Evangelical and orthodox postmillennialists will do well to steer clear of such rationalistic, destructive, sceptical and unscriptural views as are set forth in this volume." And yet this is the book which is recommended in the above review for English-speaking Chinese and for translation as "clear, concise, convincing and constructive."

As another illustration of the trend toward Modernism in China, I wish to call attention to a matter which seems to me of very great importance. In 1919, a Conference of Y. W. C. A. secretaries was held in Sungkiang, and it was addressed by a leading missionary of the Southern Presbyterian Church, Dr. J. Leighton Stuart, President of the New University at Peking, who took a series on the "World's Basis" of the Y. W. C. A. The first address was on "God", and among several points which cannot fairly be called evangelical or true to the full teaching of the New Testament are these words:

If revelation is permanent and universal, then we must admit that the Christian religion is not the only religion. It is unique in its quality, degree, purpose, completeness, and we believe it is in God's intention to be the final revelation. The Christian religion is the fullest, the finest and the final revelation, but not different in kind from the revelation of earlier ages, when you get down to the reality through the incrustations of the outside.

Jesus gave us no theory about God, no doctrine, no evidence of His existence.

There is surely something lacking here, because with statements which are true there are also others that are seriously inadequate, even to the point of error.

The second address was on "Jesus Christ," and among other statements are the following:

Jesus probably had no mystical theories about his relation to God. . . . It was a moral relationship to God. Jesus was conscious of his filial attitude; he knew he felt toward God as a son ought to feel towards his father, and that God felt that way toward him.

It is not irreverent when I say we can best understand the meaning of the human and divine when we experience it through our own persons. It is different in degree but not in kind.

It seems to me the old creedal statements no longer meet the case. To talk about two natures, two wills, etc., as though the divine and the human were separate things, is something impossible for us today. To retain them is to retain them because of a sense or attitude of loyalty, but finds no response in our own way of thinking. Can there be nature apart from personality? Does it not all belong to a type of thinking that we have long since gotten away from?

We are personalities in the process of making. God is perfect personality and he is expressed within the limitations of human life. When human character becomes perfect, then is the revelation of God perfect. In proportion as we have the life of God controlling our affections and minds will we become perfect revelations of God, just as we are now imperfect revelations of God.

Jesus revealed man in proportion as He revealed God.

Here, again, it is obvious to all who know the New Testament that the teaching concerning Christ is not only inadequate but inaccurate. Surely if there is one thing in Scripture clearer than another, it is the uniqueness of Christ, that He was different from man, not only in degree but in kind. It is, of course, easy to criticise the old statements about two natures, etc., but it is not so easy to provide an adequate substitute, and certaintly neither the lecturer nor any other modern thinker has hitherto been able to do this.

The third address was on "The Holy Spirit," and with much that is admirable there is not a little that is seriously out of harmony with New Testament teaching. What are we to say of this statement of the doctrine of the relation of the Father to the Son?

God the Father, God who had to be because he was personality in perfection; had to know that he existed; conscious of himself and his possibilities, in a certain way thought of himself objectively, God the Son. Do you find a suggestion along that line? We humans think of ourselves; there is the ego, and then each one of us, especially when he is most alive, has a distinct consciousness of his personality.

Is it not curious and really unthinkable to say that God "had to be," because He was personality in perfection, and "had to know" that He existed, and that this objective consciousness of Himself was "God the Son"? One other reference to the Trinity is the following:

Has not one trouble been that it has been an attempt to harmonize a lot of Bible texts and work out theology, rather than to find something that would help people live, and is it not better to let the doctrine go altogether than to have it as a sort of intellectual harmonizing of Bible texts that to our Western mind seem to call for some explanation?

Another lecture was on "The Holy Scriptures," and among other points that are decidedly open to objection, or, at any rate, stand in need of careful qualification, are these statements:

> The very word Bible comes by a kind of accident; Biblia can be a feminine singular noun, or can be a neuter plural noun, and from the first it has been thought of as one book. If in some way we could have kept it plural as it should have been, it would probably have done a good deal to avoid misunderstanding. People have thought of it as one book, partly due to a mistake in declension.
>
> The canon we have may include books not essential and there may be books outside that would be worth having. Some of the time we spend in reading books in the Old Testament we might spend in reading other books that might just as well be in the Bible.
>
> There is a certain feeling that we must have some infallible authority. The source of authority is the individual religious conscience. The authority of the Bible is in our own experience of its value in our own spiritual life, reinforced by religious teachers through all ages.[6]

It is obvious that these statements about the Bible are subversive of any objective authority which we can attribute to Scripture as the Word of God. If the inspiration of the Bible does not imply some unique influence of the Holy Spirit as distinct from His work of illumination today, it is difficult to know why we should ever have regarded the Bible as unique in character and of Divine authority.

Reviewing this teaching, I do not hesitate to say that it is not safe teaching to give to the Y. W. C. A. secretaries, or, indeed, to anyone else, in China or in America. When my friend and fellow-traveller, Mr. Trumbull, suggested to a missionary that the one who gave these lectures was not trustworthy in his doctrinal position, the statement was met by an almost indignant denial, on the ground that the lecturer was thoroughly true to the Deity of Christ and

---

[6] All these quotations are taken from the *Annual Report* of the Conference, and the following statement is made in it with regard to the Addresses: "This is merely a stenographic report and is undoubtedly faulty in places."

in his personal devotion to our Lord. But, even so, I will dare to say that this claim to loyalty to the Deity of Christ does not justify him in propagating such statements as I have quoted, which are manifest denials of the truth of Scripture concerning God and Christ.

The serious inadequacy and essential inaccuracy of the statements are in line with not a little that I heard in China, which gave me the impression of undue concession. Thus, one leading missionary said that there was much in Confucianism which we Christians can preserve and use, and he quoted in support of his contention, "I came not to destroy but to fulfill." No doubt there is much that is good and right and true in Confucianism, but it may be questioned whether that text, referring as it does specifically to a Divine even though partial revelation of God, the Old Testament, can be properly applied to Confucianism. Be sides, another text tells us of something else that Christ came to do: "The Son of God was manifested that He might destroy the works of the devil"; and I failed to hear much about the particular features of Christianity which are opposed to Confucianism and Buddhism. An American professor, formerly a missionary in China, whom I heard lecture on Buddhism, said that "our spiritual foundations are not so safe as they were a few years ago." I confess I felt greatly tempted to ask him what these foundations were and why they are not so safe as they used to be.

I wish now to adduce testimonies from missionaries themselves in support of my contentions. I have already referred to the paper by the Rev. Henry E. Anderson of Hong-Kong. In addition to what has preceded, the following letter which I received from a missionary may be introduced:

I have just read your article published in The Sunday School Times of April 23rd. Please permit one who has spent about nineteen years as a missionary in China, to express his appreciation of what you have said in regard to missions as you found them in China. . . . I fully appreciated what you say in regard to the over-emphasis that is being put on educational work, and at the expense of evangelistic work. I have seen this evil growing for a number of years, more especially during the last ten. We all recognize the very great importance of education, and especially in the training of a Christian ministry. But the trouble is, that multitudes of young men and women in China are wanting education of a purely secular character, and in some cases an education of that kind has resulted in nothing more than sharpening of their wits, and left them without any definite standard of morals. Such a person is a greater power for evil than if he had not been educated. Our own mission has taken a definite stand against allowing education, either literary or medical, to usurp the place that we believe the Gospel ought to have in dealing with the Chinese.

I was also greatly pleased to see your attitude in regard to the Higher Criticism menace in China. Really, I cannot understand what some men whom I know, are in China for. They have no message for a heathen people such as the Chinese, for if the Bible be not what we claim for it, what is there in it for them than for any of the rest of us? The men who have done, and are now doing, the evangelistic work in China are orthodox in their belief. Higher Critics are not bringing men to Christ. But how can they? I think you have done a great service in calling the minds of thoughtful people in this country to the two great evils in the work of missions in China today. The situation needs to be known, and one who writes from your standpoint, not from that of a missionary, will find a readier hearing. But is it not a pity that missionaries in China have to start in waging a warfare with these evils, when we all ought to be waging a warfare against a common enemy?

Another missionary writes as follows about his own personal experience:

I was in Shanghai this week to see a gentleman who works independent of all mission boards, and he tells me that things are getting very bad all over China, and it seems to me from what I see that it is so. It will not be long before we will have no message to give, and if we have, no one to spread it for lack of Spirit-filled men! The seminaries are being filled with men who are New Theology men and who have no message to give. The students are being filled with rubbish and then expected to preach, and what will they preach? One seminary within a few miles teaches that there is no personal Satan and that there is little that Christ can do but be a good example. What message will their men have? None. Another group are circulating the "Literary Reconstruction of the Bible." What message can men have who have no foundation in Scripture? Everything is hue and cry for Union, "get together, drop your differences and rally around your agreements," when every sane man knows that men of conviction and men with messages stress differences. I was all broken up over a student conference in which I was supposed to play a part. I was sponsor for delegates, and when they came together I was present as much as I could be. One of my co-workers spent all his time there, and there was not a thing taught or said that could not have been as well taught and said about Confucious. He got up and protested and was "sat on," and when I took it up with the Y. M. C. A. man who was in charge he spoke severely and said that they were tired of this old Pharisee business. I was, of course, the Pharisee. Well, so it goes. Only a few of the "Y." men out here are men who stand for sound doctrine and sound thinking. It is a keen disappointment that so many of them are so loose in their beliefs. What is to be the outcome? If the battle line is built on shifting sand how can the siege be won?

I now give extracts from a letter which I received while in China from a missionary who is very well known:

I will give some proofs which will show that the Bible is attacked in the Christian institutes of China. Two years ago, a Chinese pastor wept as he told me that a graduate of Union Seminary, New York, was teaching a class of leaders. He rejected the Virgin Birth, the Resurrection, and the Inspiration of the Scriptures. When we quoted Scripture to refute his error he got angry and told us that our attainments did not entitle us to question what "all scholarship" in the West had accepted. At that time that missionary was teaching in an important Union College.

Last year I was holding meetings at a large school in one of our provincial capitals when one of the Chinese teachers said: "Your teaching re the Bible is not the same as that given by one of the professors at the ——— University. On enquiry I found that the professor in question was a disciple of Kent, author of the notorious "Shorter Bible." This young teacher, fortunately, had not absorbed the poison and said he stood with me for a whole Bible.

Less than a year ago two missionaries told me that when their students came back from the union college which their mission had joined they said they were not sure that such a man as Moses ever had existed. They were Southern Presbyterians and were strongly of the opinion that they should withdraw from such a college.

This year in K——— Province, a young Chinese pastor, a recent graduate of ——— ——— Theological College, at the close of a ten days' series of meetings testified with deep feeling, saying:

"I graduated from college only accepting the words of Jesus as inspired; all else was no more inspired than any other writings. Now, thank God, my Bible from Genesis to Revelation has been restored." At the close of a series of meetings in K——— another graduate from the same college gave an almost identical testimony. How idiotic and wicked that men in the schools of the prophets will spend years in filling students with that which can be knocked out by the truth in a few days!

Later I was invited by the principal of that college to give sixteen addresses to the forty theological students then in attendance. The principal never missed a meeting and the students could see he was in full sympathy. The one who is reported as having said he was going to counteract what I had taught by teaching the very opposite did not attend a single meeting. He will have some difficulty in showing the students that what I taught was not scriptural.

It was quite manifest that the poison of unbelief had entered the hearts of the students, for as soon as I spoke on the integrity of the Bible many of the students showed supreme contempt, as much as to say, "Well, you are a back number, etc.," but as the days passed it lessened and in the end disappeared. At the testimony meeting on the last night the Chinese teacher or professor said: "At first I found myself objecting to many things, but in the end all objections were swept away and I saw myself as the chief of sinners, etc., etc." Since then a friend of his said his life had been transformed.

The brightest student in the college, due to graduate his year, said: "Before these meetings I had decided to go into politics and drop preaching, but these days the Spirit of God has searched me through and through, and now, if I starve, I will preach the Gospel all my days." Not to be tedious, I may say that the trend of all the testimonies was thus. Before these meetings we looked forward to preaching as a well-nigh hopeless task but now we believe that all things are possible to men filled with the Spirit of God and relying on His word. The harvest is plenteous and the labourers are few, and this criticism of the Word of God is unfitting the reapers who do come out to the harvest field.

These are the words of another leading missionary, writing to a friend of mine in America:

Dr. Thomas has doubtless told you something of the effects of such destructive propaganda, but it might be well to give in addition an extract from a recent letter of Dr. Fitch's to our New York Secretaries. "I believe that the time has come when the need of guarding the purity of the faith on the mission field ought to be shown. Time forbids more than the mentioning of an instance or two. Dr. Tewksbury of the China Sunday School Union, reported that he picked up a student's lecture notes in a certain large mission school and found in it that the miracles of Jesus were divided into three classes. Of the first it was said: 'These miracles are without historical foundation'; of the second: 'These miracles are doubtful'; of the third: 'These miracles may be accepted as genuine.'"

At the Pei-tai-ho Summer Conference in 1920, Rev. Ting Li Mei, the man noted all over China for his evangelistic zeal, said to some of his old Shantung schoolmates and friends that he was greatly troubled about his duty. He did not know whether he should continue longer where he was or not, for in the Summer and other conferences in which he was assisting there were men who taught that Jesus was only a man, and that the whole point of His life lay in His example. I have in my possession reports of such a summer conference which show that such things have been said. This shows why throughout China such a strong purpose is being aroused to prevent all the theological schools being organized on the basis of liberal theology.[7]

That this trouble is by no means recent in China may be proved by the following extract from a missionary who has been in China for some years:

Years ago I deeply felt that such a division amongst missionaries as pointed out by you was bound to come. I attended the last Centenary Conference at Shanghai, 1907, and since then I have had increased conviction that those who stand for "the faith once for all delivered" one day will have to oppose the ever-increasing body of modern missionaries who are propagating a twentieth century Gospel. Those who stand for the historic faith of evangelical Christianity will have my hearty sympathy and energetic support as soon as I have returned to China.

The same serious condition of things is implied in a recent circular letter from a well-known medical missionary, Dr. Duncan Main of Hangchow, who writes as follows:

In these days of so much talk about social service, reconstruction methods, this and that reform, swollenheadism, Bolshevik ideas, Buddhistic principles, Confucian ethics, we have to beware of Satan coming in among us as an angel of light, and we must be able to recognize the symptoms and diagnose the trouble, and more and more consider the Lord Jesus lest we become distracted and sluggish and lose our powers of resistance, and so become inadequate to the task we have been sent out to do, and slack in contending earnestly for "the faith once for all delivered to the saints." It is good for us not to forget to reaffirm our faith in the whole Bible as the inspired Word of God, and the ultimate source of authority for Christian faith and practice. Unless the Bible is believed to be the Revelation of God, and Jesus Christ is proclaimed as the only Saviour of the world, missions cannot possibly receive the blessing of God. They may be civilizing agencies but the war has proved to us that civilization without God may very easily be a curse instead of a blessing.[8]

---

[7] I refrain from giving the names of these writers, because, though the letters are not marked private, I have not asked permission to quote their words. But I have no doubt I could obtain this sanction if the truth of their words should be challenged.

[8] From one of his recent weekly circular letters sent to friends and helpers.

Last Spring a letter came to a friend of mine from a leading missionary in China telling him of a professor of Nanking University who gave an address at the community service held for the missionaries. At the close of the service another missionary got up and protested against the Bible being thus "torn to pieces."

Not so long ago some American women connected with certain mission boards were over in China, and they proposed that the word "evangelist" should be dropped, because, they said, in America it was associated with men like Moody, Torrey and Chapman; and they proposed that the term "social evangelist" be used instead. A Chinese missionary pointed out the impossibility of this because the word "social" in Chinese has an entirely different connotation. They also urged that workers in China should take care not to upset the faith of young girls by teaching them about hell, which, these ladies said, was not believed in in America!!

The trouble has gone in some cases far beyond mere concession. Two proposals had already been made before last summer, to translate into Chinese that deplorable book, *The Shorter Bible,* and although up to the present these efforts have been frustrated, many missionaries fear that fresh attempts will be made in the near future and will be successful.

When I tried to discover the cause of the critical teaching which I observed in almost every one of the twelve different places I visited and among missionaries of practically all the denominations. I was told that it was largely due to the kind of men sent out from some American seminaries. One missionary who several years ago went to one of these institutions heard so much that was objectionable that, to use his own words, he was compelled to go to a rescue mission to "work it off."

One instance of the way some speak and teach was given by Mr. Robert Gillies, of Shansi at a meeting of the English Bible League, held in London in the summer of 1920:

Just before I left China I went to a social meeting of the missionaries of Shanghai. The night on which I was there the Society had invited the leading Zionist, a prominent Jewish citizen of Shanghai, to tell to the missionary community his ideas about the return of the Jews to Palestine. It was very grand to hear that devout man citing the prophets as he spoke with such enthusiam and patriotism of the speedy fulfillment of many of these prophecies of the Old Testament. After he had finished there was discussion, and one's heart was saddened to hear one missionary after another stand up and either ridicule or ignore the idea of the Old Testament prophecies having a future fulfillment, and to realize that only a small proportion of that representative gathering held to the infallibility of the Bible.[9]

One regrettable feature is that missionaries have been told, as young people are often given the impression at home, that all scholarship is on the critical side, and that no scholar worthy of the name takes the conservative view. The missionaries have heard this so often that they have apparently almost come to believe it. Were it not so serious it would be a reminder of the word of the author of *Alice in Wonderland*, who makes one of his characters say, "What I tell you three times is true." But mere reiteration can not make a thing true.

When I showed in some of my addresses that there is not a little to be said for conservative scholarship I was charged with "dividing the missionaries," though the real division had been caused by the promulgation of the new and erroneous critical teaching. So long as conservatives are silent there is "union," and meanwhile the other side propagate their views. But when conservatives speak out they are "divisive."

One missionary said she would rather send her girls to a non-Christian school than to some of the so-called Christian schools in China, and another wrote to a friend asking earnest prayer for her girls as they went from the interior to a missionary educational institution. The missionary added that she would just as soon let her girls go to America with all the risks attending that step.

This is not surprising in view of existing conditions.

[9] *Bible League Quarterly*, July, 1920.

One of the missionaries gave me a copy of "a paper prepared by a young lady volunteer for China" which he had printed for private use because he regarded it, I believe rightly, as being "a fair sample of the training the many volunteers in Union Theological Seminary, New York, are receiving during their preparation for foreign fields." He introduced the "paper" which is here reproduced in full, with the following brief explanation: "The expression 'categories of thought' is used several times in this paper, and a few instances of contrast between Biblical categories of thought and modern categories of thought are given so that there may be a clear understanding of the meaning of words":

CONTRASTING CATEGORIES OF THOUGHT

Biblical	*Modern*
1. The earth was thought of as being flat, and the centre of the universe, which was so small that it could be measured in all directions.	1. The earth is thought of as spherical, as revolving about the sun, a part of the universe, unthinkably large.
2. Sickness was thought of as being caused by spirits and demons.	2. Sickness is thought of as being caused by germs, mainly.
3. In regard to apocalyptic hopes, there was pessimism about the present, the Kingdom of God was future, coming soon and suddenly.	3. Apocalyptic hopes look to a gradual progress of the divine growing out in man. Faith in God is necessary that the culmination may be hopeful.
4. Belief in miracle as a violation of a fixed system or as the work of a superhuman king.	4. Belief in law. So-called miracles of today are God's use of law-abiding forces to work out in ways surprising to us His will for our lives.

I

PRESENT ATTITUDES CAUSING A PROBLEM

(a) Among missionaries.

1. The majority of missionaries live partly in modern and partly in Biblical categories of thought, and teach literal belief in Bible as based on categories.
2. The majority of missionaries are intolerant of higher criticism and of the teaching of modern views for fear of faith being destroyed.
3. The minority of missionaries live in modern categories of thought and change emphasis from literal belief in Bible based on the old categories to vital teachings based on modern categories.

(*b*) Among Chinese.

1. The majority of Chinese Christians live in Biblical categories of thought and teach literal belief in the Bible.
2. The majority of Chinese Christians are ignorant of higher criticism and modern categories.
3. The minority of Chinese Christians live in modern categories of thought and change emphasis from literal belief in the Bible to vital teachings.
4. Chinese students and some Chinese churches are gaining a growing knowledge of science, which means that they will live in changed categories of thought.
5. Chinese students returned from study in America have a knowledge of the situation there and they are alive to the problem.

QUESTIONS

1. Is this description of attitudes true in all parts of China?
2. Is the liberal question an educational one or not?
3. Must the East go through the same experiences as the West, or is it possible to attempt a change of emphasis now, so that unfortunate experiences may be avoided?
4. What are the difficulties and dangers of teaching liberal views and of changing emphasis?

II.

SUGGESTED SOLUTION OF THE PROBLEM THROUGH RELIGIOUS EDUCATION

(*a*) Study of portions of the Bible with

1. Emphasis on content and message and human experience common to all ages rather than on form or terms in which the experience is recorded.
2. Emphasis on the deeds of characters in the Bible rather than on showing how they exemplify a virtue. This is sounder pedagogy; goodness in general not sufficient; must always be expressed in deeds. So a study of deeds is more satisfactory and more easily understood by children.

(*b*) Study of the spirit of the Bible as shown by

1. History of the Hebrews.
2. Life of Hebrews in contrast with that of other nations.
3. Writings of the Hebrews in contrast with writings of other nations.

(*c*) Study of the history of records—how the Bible came to be.

(*d*) Study of the uses of the Bible in past centuries: (1) Among Hebrews, (2) among Christians.

(*e*) Study of contrasting categories of thought between Biblical times and the present time.

(*f*) Study of the whole Bible, emphasizing roadways from Genesis to Revelation, showing the growing thought in regard to ideas of God, of righteousness, of worship, of sin, of faith, of prayer, etc.

(g) Study of the Christian religion as best meeting the needs of man, and as being the foundation of democratic ideals.

(h) Study of how to pass on our religious inheritance to the children.

QUESTIONS

1. Would it be possible or advisable for missionaries to follow any such course, in their private study of the Bible, without a teacher?

2. Would there be a deeper reverence for the Bible if faith and intellect could both approve the truths found there?

3. In America, where the problem has been present a longer time, many are turning away from the Bible entirely. Should the church seek for liberal teachers to rebuild the values of the Bible for them, or should it let them go?

4. Will the church be ready, if this situation should some day come to China? What can the church do to get ready?

5. How to avoid mere intellectualism and lack of fervor which too frequently accompany liberal views?

BIBLIOGRAPHY

Hunting—The Story of our Bible.
Fosdick—The Meaning of Prayer.
    "   The Meaning of Faith.
Coe—A Social Theory of Religious Education.
    "   Psychology of Religion.
Fosdick—The Use of the Bible in Teaching and Preaching.
Coe—Psychology of the Christian Life.
    "   Theory of Religious Education.
Sailer—Problems in Missionary Education.
McMurry—Criticism and Supervision of Instruction in Elementary Schools, with reference to methods of teaching.
Patrick—Industrial Arts in the Elementary Grades.
Tallman—The Teaching of Religion.
    "   The Use of the Bible in Religious Education.
Kenyon and Stewart—Health Problems of Religious and Social Workers.
Articles in Religious Education Magazine.
Courses in Teachers' College and Union Seminary.

To say nothing of the point of view here adopted, it will be observed that the bibliography is almost wholly one-sided.

Another illustration of the same tendency is recorded in *The Religious Herald* of September 30, 1920, a Baptist paper published at Richmond, Va. A young man, a graduate of a Baptist college and of a Baptist theological seminary, was among those under examination. One of the examiners said to him: "You are offering to go among a heathen people to preach the Gospel of Christ. What do you think of Him? Is He Divine?" Without a moment's hesitation the young candidate for the foreign field answered: "He is Divine just as you and I are Divine, no more, no less." A lively discussion followed and there was outspoken opposition to the appointment, but the majority of the examining committee voted to send him.

To the same effect a missionary in China writes home: "It makes one's heart ache to know and hear what is being taught in our schools in China. One of the teachers in the theological department of the university disputed the deity of Christ and—what naturally follows or goes with it —the inspiration of the Bible, etc., and he is only one of many."

One thing has greatly surprised me in connection with this subject. In several quarters the impression has been given that my criticism of missions is something new, a revelation of a condition of things that did not exist before last year. But the reverse is the fact as I can easily prove. In the May number of *The Moody Bible Institute Monthly* the Editor remarked that he could not see why I should be criticised, because I have "said nothing which has not been common report in this country for a decade at least."

Another testimony to the same effect is seen in the resolution that was unanimously adopted at the series of three meetings held under the auspices of the Bible League in London in June, 1920, that date being, of course, before I had even landed in China. These meetings of the English League were for the sole purpose of expressing "great concern as to the bearing of Destructive Criticism of the Bible on Missionary Work." This is the resolution:

RESOLVED—That this interdenominational gathering of Christians, moved to deep concern as to the bearing of Destructive Criticism of the Bible on Missionary Work, and praying that the Word of the Lord may run and be glorified in all parts of the world, earnestly begs Missionary Societies, and especially the Candidates' Committees of these Societies, to exercise constant watchfulness against the sending forth as Missionaries of any who deny or doubt that every writing of the

Old and New Testaments is God-breathed, through men who spake from God, being moved by the Holy Ghost.[10]

In a book entitled *Missionary Joys in Japan,* by Paget Wilkes, an Oxford graduate who has been over twenty years in Japan, the last chapter is entitled "Higher Criticism and the Mission Field." The book was published more than ten years ago, and as far back as 1914 I received a letter enclosing a booklet containing the last chapter of Mr. Wilkes' book and inviting me to get it distributed among Christian students. The writer remarked that "we think the sad facts may touch a true Christian who may be in danger of being led on these lines." Although Mr. Wilkes' book necessarily refers to Japan, his words have a very definite application to China, and I cannot do better than give a quotation, even though it is somewhat lengthy, from this book.

For sixteen years I have been labouring in this country, and have travelled many thousands of miles, in all directions, met missionaries of all denominations, seen all kinds of work, mixed with Christians of all classes and persuasions, and have never yet seen or heard of any individual or any body of Christians brought nearer to Christ, and made more earnest or intelligent workers in His Kingdom, through the influence of Modern Criticism. I have, on the contrary, seen and heard of many bewildered, deceived and spiritually ruined thereby. It is the consensus of opinion among the most earnest workers that wherever it comes it brings blight and paralysis into the churches. The present condition of weakness and lack of evangelistic zeal and devotion can unquestionably be traced in some large degree to its desolating influences.

In conclusion, I might add that in my judgment the more moderate school of Criticism is the more dangerous of the two—for inasmuch as a little knowledge is a dangerous thing, the less extreme views lack, as it seems to me, the foundation of real solid thinking and tend to divert the mind from the problems concerned and the real issues at stake; and so, while satisfying it with supposed solutions of mere surface and textual difficulties, rather hide the evil of that modern apostasy which denies that there is any qualitative distinction between Natural and Revealed Religion.

It is not long before the honest and more thoughtful mind, finding itself dissatisfied with a mere superficial explanation of things, makes its way into the deeper jungle of Destructive Criticism, there to lose,

---

[10] *Bible League Quarterly,* July, 1920.

and in some cases forever, all its confidence in God and His salvation.

The only hope is that the day is not far distant when the spiritual laity of our home countries, who give so liberally to the support of God's work in heathen lands, will make a strict and searching inquiry as to what is being proclaimed in the name of the Everlasting Gospel, and yet which is, alas, in some cases so far removed from its spirit and its truth.

Since the preparation of this article Mr. D. E. Hoste, Director of the China Inland Mission, has written giving his reasons for joining the Bible Union of China, and this testimony coming from so careful, able and balanced an authority not only carries deserved weight, but conclusively proves my contentions as to the fact and serious consequences of Modernism in China.

In a recent number of *The Missionary Review of the World* a significant incident was told as to the kind of missionaries needed in China:

> Three Chinese Christian leaders were talking with the Rev. George T. Scott, one of the Secretaries of the Presbyterian Board of Foreign Missions. They were Mr. David Yui, Chinese Secretary of the Young Men's Christian Association, Rev. Chung Ching Yi, Secretary of the "China for Christ Movement," and Mr. Fong Sec, head of the Commercial Press of Shanghai.
>
> "What kind of missionaries does China need?" asked Mr. Scott. The three leaders thought a moment and then replied emphatically:
>
> "*A missionary to China must have a deep conviction on Christian fundamentals... No foreigner can win us to a belief in what he only half believes.*"

I have felt it necessary to criticise much that I saw and heard in China, but in spite of everything I have three strong grounds for hope. The first is the fact that, as far as the older generation is concerned, the Chinese take the Bible as they find it and accept it simply and beautifully as it is in truth, the Word of God. They believe that Scripture says what it means and means what it says. The result is that they are usually without the difficulties which we in the Occident sometimes feel, although my experience of answering their questions showed how alert the Chinese mind is. But it is a great thing, and one that will take criticism some time to set aside, that most of the older

Chinese Christians regard the Bible as the authoritative and inspired Word of God. The peril is to the younger generation.

Another ground for hope is due to the fact that Higher Critical teaching does not produce spiritual results in China any more than it does here. As an English evangelist once said, "German theology is no use in a revival." Here is one instance in proof that Modernism is really sterile. It was told at a meeting in London of the English Bible League, and I reproduce it from the magazine:

> In the province of Shansi, in China, there is a Bible training school. The students heard that Dr. Hastings' Bible Dictionary was being translated into Chinese. So eager were they to get all the help they could in Bible study that they saved up their money to buy it as soon as it was out. The books arrived, the students received their sets of volumes with the greatest enthusiasm and went to their rooms to study their new possessions and to hunt up various subjects on which they wanted light. The next day the missionary found himself in a difficulty. The men came to him and said, "The Bible says so and so, the Dictionary says differently. What are we to do?" The missionary offered to buy back the volumes at half price, and together they would burn the lot. It was a touching sight to see those young Chinamen handing in the volumes to be burned, for a nice looking book is dear to the heart of a Chinaman![11]

I rejoice to know that the late Professor James Orr's *International Standard Bible Encyclopaedia* is being adapted for Chinese use.

But my greatest ground for hope lies in the formation of the Bible Union of China, particulars of which have already been given.

And now I want to make three suggestions. The first is that people at home should be informed regarding *all* that is going on in China. It is for this reason that I am telling my experiences. Similarly, Mr. Rankin, the American lawyer to whom I referred above, has felt it his duty by speech and pen to inform the laymen of his denomination to what lengths the Higher Critical trouble has gone.

The next suggestion I make is that everyone should do

---

[11] *Bible League Quartely*, July, 1920.

what is possible to influence the foreign missionary boards of the denominations to send out only the right men. One missionary told me how sad and unsatisfactory had been his experience as one of only two men at a station, the other being an exponent of the Higher Criticism. There was and could be no fellowship and no real coöperation between them. If Dr. J. Wilbur Chapman's suggestion is impossible,—that of recalling from the field all the missionaries who have ceased to believe the Bible to be authoritative, —at least the missionary boards, or whatever church authority has this jurisdiction, should prevent any more such from going out. Since my return I have read of Home Committees passing two men who did not believe, one in the Virgin Birth, and the other in the unique Deity of Christ. And I wish to say most emphatically that it is no mere question of whether a majority or a minority of missionaries hold the views which the evangelical Christian church regards as wrong. The matter is far more serious; for the issue is as to why any missionary at all holding the critical views of the Bible should be sent to the foreign field.

My third suggestion is that we do our best to provide missionaries with the best books on the conservative side. I found that several books, well-known in home lands, were absolutely unknown there, and I mentioned several of these to one of the leading workers engaged in translational work. Missionaries are often not able to buy works, even if they know them, owing to the high cost of books when purchased in China. People of means could not do anything better with their money than to provide these noble workers with books of the right sort which fortify mind and heart.

In an article on "The Future of Religion in China," which appeared in the *Atlantic Monthly* for January last, the writer, a missionary whom I met in Shanghai, says that the missionaries have gone out to China very largely to vindicate Western civilization, and that their task is nearer accomplishment than most of them realize. This is interesting, but it is not true; and I could not have a better proof of the weakness of a good deal of Chinese missionary work than that article. Our sound missionaries have gone to China to proclaim the everlasting Gospel of a crucified, risen and personal Saviour from sin, and not to vindicate any civilization. There is much in Western civilization which, because it is not Christian, is not worth vindication, and that missionary writer's statement of the purpose of missionary work is not only inadequate but wrong. Christianity is Christ, and civilization is not necessarily Christianity. Christianity means the Gospel, and the Gospel means redemption from sin; and it behooves those at home and those abroad to seek to proclaim by lip and life the message of that Gospel as "the power of God unto salvation to every one that believeth."

Philadelphia, Pa.   W. H. GRIFFITH THOMAS.

MODERNISM

AND

THE BOARD OF FOREIGN MISSIONS

OF THE PRESBYTERIAN CHURCH

IN THE U. S. A.

———

ARGUMENT OF J. GRESHAM MACHEN IN SUP-
PORT OF AN OVERTURE INTRODUCED IN THE PRES-
BYTERY OF NEW BRUNSWICK AT ITS MEETING ON
JANUARY 24, 1933, AND MADE THE ORDER OF
THE DAY FOR THE MEETING ON APRIL 11, 1933.

THE PROPOSED OVERTURE

The Presbytery of New Brunswick respectfully overtures the General Assembly of 1933,

1. To take care to elect to positions on the Board of Foreign Missions only persons who are fully aware of the danger in which the Church stands and who are determined to insist upon such verities as the full truthfulness of Scripture, the virgin birth of our Lord, His substitutionary death as a sacrifice to satisfy Divine justice, His bodily resurrection and His miracles, as being essential to the Word of God and our Standards and as being necessary to the message which every missionary under our Church shall proclaim,

2. To instruct the Board of Foreign Missions that no one who denies the absolute necessity of acceptance of such verities by every candidate for the ministry can possibly be regarded as competent to occupy the position of Candidate Secretary,

3. To instruct the Board of Foreign Missions to take care lest, by the wording of the application blanks for information from candidates and from those who are asked to express opinions about them, or in any other way, the impression be produced that tolerance of opposing views or ability to progress in spiritual truth, or the like, is more important than an unswerving faithfulness in the proclamation of the gospel as it is contained in the Word of God and an utter unwillingness to make common cause with any other gospel whether it goes under the name of Christ or not,

4. To warn the Board of the great danger that lurks in union enterprises at home as well as abroad, in view of the widespread error in our day.

THE INVESTIGATION OF THE BOARD.

This Argument presents specific charges against the Board of Foreign Missions of the Presbyterian Church in the U. S. A. It was sent, before the meeting of Presbytery, to all the ministers and elders in the Presbytery, to all the members and secretaries of the Board of Foreign Missions and to Rev. Professor Daniel Johnson Fleming, Ph.D., D.D., of the Presbytery of New York. By express invitation of the Presbytery, Dr. Robert E. Speer, Senior Secretary of the Board, was present at the meeting.

At the meeting, I pointed out that Dr. Speer himself had signed, in 1932, a Report of the Committee on Coöperation in Latin America, which mentioned among "the outstanding accomplishments of the Book Department" the securing of the publication in Spanish of "several books by Dr. Harry Emerson Fosdick and other American authors,"(1) although the divergence of Dr. Fosdick's teaching from the Bible and from the faith of the Presbyterian Church is perfectly well known.

Dr. Speer, in his address, made no answer at all to this representation, and practically no answer to any of the other specific charges against the Board, stating that he did not desire to engage in controversy. In accordance with this expressed desire of Dr. Speer, the previous question was moved very soon after the speeches were over, and debate was thus soon shut off. The Overture was then defeated by a *viva voce* vote, and another motion expressing confidence in the Board of Foreign Missions was passed. The temper of Presbytery was obviously opposed to anything like real debate on this second motion.

I dissented from the procedure shutting off debate. No sensible person can have confidence in a Board which does not welcome open discussion of its policies with those to whom it appeals for funds. As a matter of fact, the Board of Foreign Missions of the Presbyterian Church in the U. S. A. is deeply involved in Modernist and destructive propaganda, and its appeal to Bible-believing Christians is a misleading appeal.

Evidence in support of this position will be found in the present Argument, which appears here in its original form except for corrections in, and improvement of, the citations from the Report of the Lakeville Conference on pp. 44, 52, 53, and one or two purely formal or orthographic corrections elsewhere.

Additional copies may be secured, free, by application to the author at 206 South Thirteenth Street, Philadelphia, Pa.

J. GRESHAM MACHEN.

April 18, 1933.

---

(1) See *Foreign Missions Conference of North America, 1932, Report of the Thirty-Ninth Annual Meeting, January, 1932*, p. 92. Dr. Speer's name is appended to the Report on page 114, as Chairman of the Committee, together with that of Samuel G. Inman, as Secretary. The Committee appears in the *Report of the Board of Foreign Missions of the Presbyterian Church in the U. S. A.*, 1932, p. 217, as part of the "Union and Coöperative Foreign Mission Work of the Presbyterian Church U. S. A."

FOREWORD.

I am presenting this Overture not because I desire to do so but because I am compelled to do so. I should be far happier if I did not know certain things about the Board of Foreign Missions of the Presbyterian Church in the U. S. A.; but I do know those things, and the knowledge of them places upon me a duty which I cannot evade. My membership in a Presbytery seems to me to be a sacred trust, and it is in discharge of the obligations of that trust that I am presenting the proposed Overture and some of the reasons which have compelled me to advocate it.

I. THE ATTITUDE OF THE BOARD OF FOREIGN MISSIONS TOWARD THE BOOK "RE-THINKING MISSIONS."

The Book "Re-Thinking Missions."

At the end of the year 1932, a book entitled "Re-Thinking Missions" was issued as the report of the "Commission of Appraisal" of the "Laymen's Inquiry after One Hundred Years." The character of the book is too well known to require extended exposition. It is exactly what was to be expected of a Commission which has as its chairman Dr. William Ernest Hocking of Harvard and includes among its members such well-known Modernists as Dr. Rufus M. Jones of Haverford and (as the only representative of our Church) Dr. William P. Merrill of New York. The work of the Commission was financed, to the extent of some half-million dollars, largely by a Modernist layman, Mr. John D. Rockefeller, Jr., who in 1918 wrote for the *Saturday Evening Post* an article which was afterwards circulated in pamphlet form[1] advocating admission to the Church without any profession of belief whatever.

The resulting book constitutes from beginning to end an attack upon the historic Christian Faith. It presents as the aim of missions that of *seeking* truth together with adherents of other religions rather than that of *presenting* the truth which God has supernaturally recorded in the Bible. "The relation between religions," it says, "must take increasingly hereafter the form of a common search for truth" (p. 47). It deprecates the distinction between Christians and non-Christians (pp. 58, 141); it belittles the Bible and inveighs against Christian doctrine (pp. 103, 102f., and *passim*); it dismisses the doctrine of eternal punishment as a doctrine antiquated even in Christendom (p. 19); it presents Jesus as a great religious Teacher and Example, as Christianity's "highest expression of the religious life," but

---

[1] John D. Rockefeller, Jr., *"The Christian Church, What of Its Future,"* reprinted from *Saturday Evening Post*, issue of February 9, 1918.

certainly not as very God of very God; it belittles evangelism, definite conversions, open profession of faith in Christ, membership in the Christian Church (p. 277), and substitutes "the dissemination of spiritual influences" (p. 100) and "the permeation of the community with Christian ideals and principles" (p. 164) for the new birth.

The Official Action of the Board.

What is the attitude of our Board of Foreign Missions toward this broadside of modern unbelief? The answer is given in an official "Action of the Board of Foreign Missions" passed November 21, 1932, and published both in *The Presbyterian Magazine*[1] and in pamphlet form.

This answer is exceedingly disquieting to Bible-believing Christians in the Presbyterian Church.

In the first place, it contains no clear pronouncement for or against the main thesis of the Appraisal Commission's Report. Yet the situation clearly demanded such a pronouncement. The Appraisal Commission had made a public attack against the very heart of the Christian religion. The attack had been made in the name of Christianity, and was, therefore, likely to deceive the rank and file of the Church. Futhermore, our Board of Foreign Missions was deeply implicated in it. Two members of the Board, Mr. James M. Speers and Mrs. John H. Finley, were members of the original Laymen's Foreign Missions Inquiry, which appointed the Appraisal Commission. Of these, Mr. Speers, a vice-president of the board, was actually Chairman of the Presbyterian Committee of the Laymen's Inquiry. Moreover, the Board had officially welcomed the Inquiry, despite its plainly anti-evangelical personnel, in the warmest terms. In its report to the 1932 General Assembly it said (p. 13) :

> "It is hoped that the result of this inquiry will be a greatly deepened interest in and support of the missionary enterprise by the lay forces of the Churches of America."

---

[1] Issue of January, 1933.

When, therefore, the Appraisal Commission's Report appeared and was issued by the Inquiry, and when it presented a very clear-cut view of what missions are and what the Christian religion is, the people of the Church had a right to know whether the Board rejected or accepted that view. Did it agree with its Vice-President, Mr. Speers, and another of its members, Mrs. Finley, in their action in issuing the Appraisal Commission's Report, or did it repudiate this action of these two of its members and pronounce the Report of the Appraisal Commission as being, what it clearly is, hostile to the roots of the Christian religion? Did it think that the hopes about the Inquiry which it had officially expressed at the 1932 General Assembly was justified by the result, or did it confess that those hopes were mistaken and had proved to be misleading to Christ's little ones in the Church?

It made no answer to these inquiries. It dodged the issue.

The Basis of Missions.

What the Board did do was to issue a vague statement about "the evangelical basis of missions"—a statement so vague that it could be acquiesced in, presumably, even by the two members of the Board who were members of the Laymen's Inquiry and even by certain unnamed members of the Appraisal Commission itself.

The Board says, in its official statement:

"The work of the Board is built on the motive described in the foreword of the Commission's Report in the words, 'To some of our members the enduring motive of Christian missions can be adequately expressed as loyalty to Jesus Christ regarded as the perfect revelation of God and the only way by which men can reach a satisfying experience of him.'"

Let us understand exactly what that means. All of the members of the Appraisal Commission, without exception, have agreed to the Appraisal Commission's Report; there was no minority report. All of them, without exception, have agreed to all of this thoroughgoing attack upon the very heart and core of Christianity. Whatever differences of opinion they may have had among themselves are expressly declared to have been consonant with agreement in the findings of the Report. "Retaining these differences," says the Foreword (p. XV), "the members of the Commission unite in the judgments set forth in this book."

Within this general agreement with the findings of this thoroughly anti-Christian book, there were, according to the Foreword, different opinions among the members concerning the aim of missions. And one of those opinions, held by persons who expressly unite in the anti-Christian propaganda of this book, is designated officially by our Board of Foreign Missions as the motive upon which the work of our Board is based! We can only say that if that be the foundation upon which the work of our Board is based, then the work of our Board is based upon shifting sand.

It is not surprising that this utterance, which represents the view of certain signers of the anti-Christian Report of the Appraisal Commission and is expressly taken to itself by our Board, is unsatisfactory even in content, to say nothing of its context in the Report. There is in it nothing about Christ as Saviour: He is treated only as a leader to whom man may be loyal, not as a Saviour in whom a man can believe; only as a revealer, not as a Redeemer. And the result of missions is designated not as the salvation of lost souls, not as the glory of God which is really man's chief end, but as merely this—to "reach a satisfying experience of Him." Could any language be more unsatisfactory to a man who has the slightest inkling of the awfulness of sin, the blessedness of redemption, the majesty of God's glory?

It is true that the Board does go on to speak of Christ as "only Lord and Saviour" and does go on to speak of Him as "Divine Redeemer." But in what studiedly vague and general terms! Did ever a trumpet in time of battle, in a time when the very citadel of the Faith had been attacked, give forth a feebler sound!

The Aim of Missions.

Here is what the Board, in its Statement, says it has long expressed in its Manual as being the aim of missions:

"The supreme and controlling aim of Foreign Missions is to make the Lord Jesus Christ known to all men as their Divine Saviour and to persuade them to become His disciples; to gather these disciples into Churches which shall be self-propagating, self-supporting, self-governing; to cooperate, so long as necessary, with the Churches in the evangelizing of their countrymen, and in bringing to bear on all human life the spirit and principles of Christ."

Where is there any reference here to the things really distinctive of Christian missions, where is there, at least, any reference to such things in terms which are not often distorted by modern unbelief to mean something entirely different from what they used to mean? Where is there any reference to the guilt of sin? Where is there any reference to eternal punishment—that solemn doctrine which is so fundamental in the words of our blessed Lord? Where is there any reference to His virgin birth, His blood shed when He offered up Himself as a sacrifice to satisfy divine justice and reconcile us to God, His bodily resurrection? Where is there any reference to the utter insufficiency of human attempts at following Jesus to present a man faultless before the judgment seat of God? Where is there any reference to the new birth? What is meant by the phrase—so dear to the Modernism of our day—"bringing to bear on human life the spirit and principles of Christ"? Does that phrase mean that there is any hope in "the principles of Christ" apart from His atoning blood, any hope in the permeation of human life with His "spirit" except as a man is begotten again by the supernatural act of the Spirit of God? How different is the Holy Spirit, who is the Spirit of our Lord Jesus Christ, the Third Person of the blessed Trinity—how different is that Spirit from the vague influence spoken of by the Board and by the Report, in the language so dear to the unbelief of our day, as "the spirit of Christ" or "the spirit of Jesus."

Let it not be said that the Board is speaking here about the aim of missions rather than about the content of the Christian message. The point is that the situation imperatively demanded a pronouncement about the content of the Christian message. The central thing in the Appraisal Commission's Report is that that Report presents a view regarding the content of the Christian message which is diametrically opposed to the view which the Bible and the Confession of Faith of the Presbyterian Church present. It was the bounden duty of our Board of Foreign Missions, in commenting upon the Report of the Appraisal Commission, to say something very definite about the content of the Christian message.

Let it not be said, further, that we must not expect too much in such a brief statement, and that if the Board had had more space it would have insisted upon many things which are not contained in this statement—would have insisted, for example, upon the necessity of belief in the virgin birth, the substitutionary atonement, the bodily resurrection, and other specific doctrines of the Word of God. No, the thing is only too plain. The Board left these things out of the statement because it *had to do so*— because it had to do so if it were to obtain the acquiescence of all its members and were thus to continue to conceal from donors the real state of affairs in that Board to which they are being asked to send their gifts. We have here in extreme form the evils of a unanimous action. The situation demanded from the Board a clear-cut decision for or against the book *Re-Thinking Missions;* for or against the Modernism of some of its own members. Instead, the Board maintained its policy of concealing the real facts. It formulated a vague statement in which it could get both Modernists and evangelicals among its members to agree, a vague statement which might be regarded by Bible-believing Christians in the Church as a repudiation of the book *Re-Thinking Missions* and which might be regarded by Modernists in the Church as tolerating the point of view which that book presents.

Then the Board proceeds to express agreement with many recommendations in the book:

> "The Board cordially recognizes many recommendations in the report of the Appraisal Commission of the Laymen's Foreign Missions Inquiry which, taken apart from its theological basis, it believes to be sound, which represent policies and judgments which the Board believes to be right, and which it has sought and will continue to seek to carry out in the work under its care."

What the Board here calls the "theological basis" of the Report and waves aside as a thing about which it expresses no opinion is really a denial of the truth of the Christian religion. There are some of us who think that that denial ought not to be thus waved aside and that it affects practically everything that the Report says from beginning to end.

In contemplating the statement of the Board as a whole, I am not surprised that the Modernists among the Board members should agree with it. It is couched in just the kind of vague language which Modernists love. But what does surprise me is that any evangelicals who may be among the Board members should agree with it. That they did so is surprising indeed. It was a time when the pathway of loyalty toward the Word of God and fairness toward contributors to the Board was perfectly plain. That pathway was quite different from the pathway upon which they chose to walk.

The disquieting effect of this action of the Board upon all Bible-believing Christians is not mitigated in the slightest by individual pronouncements by Dr. Robert E. Speer and other representatives of the Board against the Report of the Appraisal Commission. Some Bible-believing Christians may regard those pronouncements as satisfactory in themselves. I do not so regard them, but that is

12

not now the point. The real point is that the more evangelical those pronouncements of Dr. Robert E. Speer and others may be, the more harm they are doing to the evangelical cause. The real question is what the Board of Foreign Missions is doing with the funds which the Bible-believing Christians, at great sacrifice, are entrusting to it. That question is answered not by individual pronouncements of Dr. Speer or anyone else but by the official decisions of the Board. Dr. Speer's eloquent pronouncements are no doubt effectual in inducing Bible-believing Christians to continue to give to the Board. But they have no more effect than the wind blowing upon the question what use the Board is making of the gifts.

The answer to that question is given only too plainly by the evasive statement with which we have just been dealing. It is given with even greater plainness in the facts which we shall presently adduce.

II. THE CASE OF MRS. J. LOSSING BUCK.

In the official list of missionaries of the Presbyterian Church in the U. S. A. submitted by the Board of Foreign Missions to the 1932 General Assembly (see Report of the Board, 1932, p. 288), there appeared the name of Mrs. J. Lossing Buck. This Mrs. J. Lossing Buck is Pearl S. Buck, author of *The Good Earth* and *Sons,* and one of the best known novelists of the present day.

Mrs. Buck's Views Regarding Missions.

Mrs. Buck's views regarding missions are expressed in an article entitled "The Laymen's Mission Report" in *The Christian Century* for November 23, 1932, and in an article entitled "Is There a Case for Foreign Missions?", in *Harpers Magazine* for January, 1933.[1]

In the former article, Mrs. Buck expresses the most enthusiastic agreement with the book *Re-Thinking Missions,* and singles out for special commendation those features

[1] The latter article has subsequently been published in pamphlet form by The John Day Company, New York.

of that book which are most obviously and diametrically opposed to the Bible. She says, for example:

> "I have not read merely a report. I have read a unique book, a great book. The book presents a masterly statement of religion in its place in life, and of Christianity in its place in religion. The first three chapters are the finest exposition of religion I have ever read" (p. 1434).

> "I think this is the only book I have ever read which seems to me to be literally true in its every observation and right in its every conclusion. * * * I want every American Christian to read this book. I hope it will be translated into every language" (p. 1434).

Mrs. Buck's Views Regarding Christianity.

In the article in *Harpers Magazine*,[1] Mrs. Buck deals more generally with missions and with the nature of the Christian religion, and what she says in both articles on this subject is in thoroughgoing conflict with the historic Christian Faith. She represents the deity of Christ as a thing accepted by some and rejected by others, but certainly not essential:

> "Some of us [Christians] believe in Christ as our fathers did. To some of us he is still the divine son of God, born of the virgin Mary, conceived by the Holy Spirit. But to many of us He has ceased to be that. * * * Let us face the fact that the old reasons for foreign missions are gone from the minds and hearts of many of us, certainly from those of us who are young" (*Harpers*, p. 150).

She rejoices in the stripping of "the magic of superstition" from Christ, and it seems perfectly clear that in the "magic of superstition" she includes the miracles of Christ

---

[1] Permission to quote from this article has kindly been granted by Mrs. Buck through her literary representative. Grateful acknowledgment is also rendered The John Day Company, who have extended their permission, and to Harper & Brothers.

and the Biblical notion of the salvation which He wrought (*Harpers*, p. 151). She intimates rather clearly that what is really essential in Christianity would remain even if it should be proved at some future time that there never lived an actual Christ:

> "Even though it is proved in some future time that there never lived an actual Christ and what we think of as Christ should some day be found as the essence of men's dreams of simplest and most beautiful goodness, would I be willing to have that personification of dreams pass out of men's minds?" (*Harpers*, p. 151).

No doubt Mrs. Buck believes that Christ did live, and no doubt she derives some stimulus from that belief. But it is perfectly possible, she thinks, for those who have never heard of Christ to live the Christian life:

> "Others live it also, many who have never heard the name of Christ; but to know the meaning of Christ's life, to know how he lived and died, is an inestimable support and help" (*Harpers*, p. 152).

She rejects directly the Bible doctrine of sin:

> "I am not inclined to blame human beings very much. I do not believe in original sin. I believe that most of us start out wanting to do right and to do good. I believe that most of us keep that desire as long as we live and whatever we do" (*Harpers*, p. 148).

She rejects the old gospel of salvation from sin and even seems to advocate the denial of religious liberty to those who preach that gospel:

> "In the old days it was plain enough. Our forefathers believed sincerely in a magic religion. They believed simply and plainly that all who did not hear

the gospel, as they called it, were damned, and every soul to whom they preached received in that moment the chance for salvation from that hell. Though heard but for a single moment, the preacher gave that soul the opportunity of a choice for eternity. If the soul paid no heed or did not believe, the preacher could not take the responsibility. He was absolved. There are those who still believe this, and if they sincerely believe, I honor that sincerity, though I cannot share the belief. I agree with the Chinese who feel their people should be protected from such superstition" (*Harpers*, p. 149).

Needless to say, Mrs. Buck agrees fully with *Re-Thinking Missions* in belittling preaching as over against what she regards—quite falsely—as living the Christian life:

"Above all, then, let the spirit of Christ be manifested by mode of life rather than by preaching. I am wearied unto death with this preaching. It deadens all thought, it confuses all issues, it is producing, in China at least, a horde of hypocrites, and in the theological seminaries a body of Chinese ministers which makes one despair for the future, because they are learning how to preach about Christianity rather than how to live the Christian life" (*Harpers*, p. 155).

It is needless to say, further, that this estimate of preaching is entirely contrary to that which is taught in the Word of God.

One thing is certainly to be said for Mrs. Buck. She is admirably clear. Her utterances are as plain as the utterances of our Board of Foreign Missions are muddled. There is nothing vague or undecided about them. She has let it be known exactly where she stands. She is opposed to the old gospel and is not afraid to say so in the presence of all the world.

Mrs. Buck and our Foreign Board.

Now the important thing for us is that this outstanding advocate of modern unbelief is a missionary of the Presbyterian Church under a Board which has a perfect ecclesiastical and legal right to dismiss her at any time. Because of her independent income from her books, she is, I believe, at present dispensing with a salary from the Board. But that does not alter the case in the slightest. She is on the list of missionaries; she is known as a missionary of our Church. With the utmost clearness, and with the most passionate enthusiasm, she has thrown herself into an attack upon the historic Christian Faith. By doing so she has raised in the most definite and public way the question whether our Board of Foreign Missions will or will not lend its name to a propaganda that is diametrically opposed to that for which the Presbyterian Church exists.

Under such circumstances, there are two courses of action which the Board of Foreign Missions may pursue.

In the first place, it may do nothing; it may hope that Mrs. Buck may be eliminated quietly in some way from the roll of missionaries without intensifying yet further the charge of intolerance which already rests upon the Christian Church.

That course of action may be financially profitable. It may conserve the gifts of the host of people in the Church who agree essentially with Mrs. Buck. From the worldly point of view, much is to be said in favor of it. But it has the disadavantage of being dishonest.

The other course of action is that of dismissing Mrs. Buck from the roll of missionaries. It is obvious that such dismissal, to be of the slightest use, would have to be public and for cause. Mrs. Buck is not an obscure person; she is one of the most famous women in all the world; her attack upon the Christian message has been conducted in the most widely read magazines. Her challenge to the Board, in other words, has been public; and the answer to it would have to be equally public. Nothing whatever, indeed, would have to be said to impugn Mrs. Buck's character or motives; but the Board would have to say plainly to all the world that it is irrevocably committed to the message which Mrs. Buck has attacked, that it does not solicit a single penny from those who agree with her, and that it cannot tolerate among its missionaries any such anti-Christian propaganda as that which she is carrying on.

That course of action might entail financial loss. It might mean the elimination of gifts coming from the Modernists who now support our Board. From the worldly point of view, much could be said against it. But it would have the advantage of being honest.

Hitherto, the Board seems to have chosen the former course of action. Mrs. Buck, so far as I know, is still on the roll of our missionaries.

But even if the Board should now dismiss her, and should do so with all the publicity which the situation demands, still it would not be able merely by so doing to regain the confidence of Bible-believing Christians in the Church. Mrs. Buck's views about missions have obviously not been formed overnight. She herself intimates very plainly that the book *Re-Thinking Missions* only expresses views which she has already held. Yet she has been allowed to continue in the foreign field by a Board which is charged with the sacred duty of seeing that its mission work is in accordance with the Constitution of the Presbyterian Church and with the Word of God. Could she have done so if the Board had not been grossly neglectful of its duty?

Moreover, there is not the slightest likelihood that Mrs. Buck stands alone in her destructive views. Her distinguished talents have merely allowed those views to become widely audible in her case. It is altogether probable that there are many like her among the missionaries under our Board. Rev. John Clover Monsma (in his booklet, *The Foreign Missionary Situation in the Presbyterian Church in the U. S. A.*, February, 1933, p. 8, to which I am indebted also in other ways) is quite justified in saying:

"Today the Board is not in a position to guarantee our church members that there are not scores upon scores of other 'Mrs. Bucks' in the field, at different stages of apostasy and doctrinal revolution."

III. THE BOARD OF FOREIGN MISSIONS AND THE AUBURN AFFIRMATION.

In 1923, the General Assembly, sitting at Indianapolis, in view of the Modernist propaganda which Dr. Harry Emerson Fosdick was carrying on (as colleague of the pastor, Dr. George Alexander, President of the Board of Foreign Missions) in the pulpit of the First Presbyterian Church of New York, issued the following evangelical pronouncement:

"1. It is an essential doctrine of the Word of God and our standards that the Holy Spirit did so inspire, guide and move the writers of Holy Scripture as to keep them from error.

"2. It is an essential doctrine of the Word of God and our standards that our Lord Jesus Christ was born of the Virgin Mary.

"3. It is an essential doctrine of the Word of God and our standards that Christ offered up Himself a sacrifice to satisfy Divine justice and to reconcile us to God.

"4. It is an essential doctrine of the Word of God and of our standards concerning our Lord Jesus Christ, that on the third day He rose again from the dead with the same body with which He suffered, with which also He ascended into heaven, and there sitteth at the right hand of His Father, making intercession.

"5. It is an essential doctrine of the Word of God as the supreme standard of our faith that our Lord Jesus showed His power and love by working mighty miracles. This working was not contrary to nature, but superior to it."

This evangelical pronouncement of the General Assembly contained no intricate or detailed doctrines and no doctrines peculiar to the Reformed Faith. It merely set forth five central verities in which the great historic branches of the Christian Church are agreed.

Yet it was attacked by a document commonly called the Auburn Affirmation, which was signed by about thirteen hundred ministers in the Presbyterian Church.

The Auburn Affirmation Attacked the Inerrancy of Scripture.

The Auburn Affirmation, in the first place, attacked directly the great basic doctrine of the full truthfulness or inerrancy of Scripture, and perverted the words of our Confession of Faith, which declares that the supreme Judge·in controversy is " the Holy Spirit speaking in the Scripture," to mean "the Spirit of God, speaking to the Christian believer" (p. 4). The Affirmation says (p. 5):

> "We hold that the General Assembly of 1923, in asserting that 'the Holy Spirit did so inspire, guide and move the writers of Holy Scripture as to keep them from error,' spoke without warrant of the Scriptures or of the Confession of Faith."

At that point, there is a clear-cut break between the signers of the Auburn Affirmation and Bible-believing Christians. Signers of the Auburn Affirmation are able to see how a book can be the Word of God and at the same time contain errors; Bible-believing Christians are unable to attain to such a degree of subtlety as that; they are simple-minded enough to think that when God speaks He speaks truth and only truth.

I do not think that any amount of fine words can conceal that fundamental cleavage. The most important thing about a building is not its superstructure but its foundation; and the foundation upon which Bible-believing Christians, as distinguished from signers of the Auburn Affirmation, build is the full truthfulness of God's Holy Word.

The Auburn Affirmation Erases the Virgin Birth and Four Other Verities from the Essential Message of the Church.

But the Auburn Affirmation went far beyond a rejection of the full truthfulness of Scripture. While professing belief in certain "facts and doctrines" expressed in the vague language often employed by non-doctrinal Modernism, it declared that not a single one of the five great verities mentioned in the General Assembly's pronouncement is essential even for the ministry:

"IV. The General Assembly of 1923 expressed the opinion concerning five doctrinal statements that each one 'is an essential doctrine of the Word of God and our standards.' On the constitutional grounds which we have before described, we are opposed to any attempt to elevate these five doctrinal statements, or any of them, to the position of tests for ordination or for good standing in our church.

"Furthermore, this opinion of the General Assembly attempts to commit our church to certain theories concerning the inspiration of the Bible, and the Incarnation, the Atonement, the Resurrection, and the Continuing Life and Supernatural Power of our Lord Jesus Christ. We all hold most earnestly to these great facts and doctrines; we all believe from our hearts that the writers of the Bible were inspired of God; that Jesus Christ was God manifest in the flesh; that God was in Christ, reconciling the world unto Himself, and through Him we have our redemption; that having died for our sins He rose from the dead and is our ever-living Saviour; that in His earthly ministry He wrought many mighty works, and by His vicarious death and unfailing presence He is able to save to the uttermost.* Some of us regard the particular theories contained in the deliverance of the General Assembly of 1923 as satisfactory explanations of these facts and doctrines. But we are united in believing that these are not the only theories allowed by the Scriptures and

---

* This sentence is printed in the Affirmation in bold-faced type.

our standards as explanations of these facts and doctrines of our religion, and that all who hold to these facts and doctrines, whatever theories they may employ to explain them, are worthy of all confidence and fellowship."

Let it not be said that the Affirmation attacked the General Assembly's pronouncement merely on technical grounds, The Affirmation does, indeed, raise the technical point that the General Assembly had no right to issue such a pronouncement. But it proceeds at once to something far more fundamental. It attacks the content of the pronouncement on its merits. It declares that not a single one of the great verities mentioned by the General Assembly of 1923 is essential; and it declares that all of the five verities are merely "theories" (among other possible theories), which some may and some may not hold to be satisfactory explanations of something else. Thus according to the Auburn Affirmation a man may be a minister in the Presbyterian Church and yet deny the full truthfulness of Scripture, the virgin birth, the substitutionary atonement to satisfy divine justice and reconcile us to God, the bodily resurrection, the miracles of our Lord. It is not merely that according to the Affirmation a minister may deny one or another of these verities. No, he may deny *all* of them, according to the Affirmation, and still be a minister in the Presbyterian Church.

The issue cannot be evaded by any plea of this or that signer of the Affirmation that he personally believes in the five verities mentioned by the General Assembly.

In the first place, no signer of the Affirmation, if he knew what he was doing when he signed the document, can believe in the first of the five verities—the full truthfulness of Scripture—for that is definitely attacked in the name of all the signers in the earlier part of the Affirmation.

In the second place, if he himself accepts this or that one of the five verities, he does so, according to the terms of the Affirmation, only in the sense that he is accepting it as one theory among other possible theories in explanation of something else. Thus, according to the Affirmation, a man may say, "I believe myself that our Lord Jesus Christ was born of the Virgin Mary"; but he also says, according to the Affirmation: "I hold that that view, that Jesus Christ was born of the Virgin Mary, is only one of the theories that the Scripture allows a man to hold in explanation of the incarnation, and I am perfectly willing to receive into the ministry of the Church a man who holds to some theory of the incarnation which does not affirm that 'our Lord Jesus Christ was born of the Virgin Mary'—which holds, for example, that Jesus was the son, by ordinary generation, of Joseph and Mary."

What a morass we find ourselves in here! It is a well-known morass, the morass of that destructive Modernism which is engulfing our Presbyterian Church, as it already has engulfed so many other churches, to the ruin of countless souls.

But the really important thing to say is that the Auburn Affirmation removes all of these five verities from the essential message which the Church, as a whole and in its corporate capacity, is to deliver to the world. We are not here discussing whether signers of the Auburn Affirmation have or have not a right to continue as ministers in the Presbyterian Church. We may hold different views about that. But the question that we are discussing is the question whether signers of the Auburn Affirmation are fit persons to be employed by the great Boards of the Church for the responsible duty of saying to the world what the essential message of the Church is. With regard to that question, I do not see how there can be any possible difference of opinion among Bible-believing Christians. Of what avail is it that individual signers of the Affirmation affirm this or that one of these verities? The important thing for us today is that all of the signers remove all of these verities from the essential message of the Church. According to all the signers of the Affirmation, the Christ which the Presbyterian Church preaches to the world was or was not born of a virgin, did or did not die as a sacrifice to satisfy Divine justice and reconcile us to God, did or did not rise from the dead with the same body with which He had suffered, did or did not work miracles. Is that the Christ in whom is not yea and nay, but in whom is yea and in whom is Amen, unto the glory of God? No, my friends, it is another Christ, not the Christ presented to us by the apostle Paul and by all the Scriptures; and a Church that proclaims that other Christ is no faithful Church of God.

A Typical Modernist Document.

Let us not deceive ourselves. The Auburn Affirmation is a typical Modernist document. It is typical in the deceptive way in which it uses general terms which many interpret in a Christian sense, but which many also interpret in a non-Christian sense. It affirms "the inspiration of the Bible, and the Incarnation, the Atonement, the Resurrection, and the Continuing Life and Supernatural Power of our Lord Jesus Christ." It declares that "the writers of the Bible were inspired of God; that Jesus Christ was God manifest in the flesh; that God was in Christ, reconciling the world unto Himself, and through Him we have our redemption; that having died for our sins He rose from the dead and is our ever-living Saviour; that in His earthly ministry He wrought many mighty works, and by His vicarious death and unfailing presence He is able to save to the uttermost." That sounds Christian, does it not? But the trouble is that every one of these noble terms is often used today in a non-Christian sense by destructive unbelief; and the Auburn Affirmation is careful to say that it will not define those terms in the manner that the General Assembly did, so as to break definitely with unbelief. A document which will affirm inspiration but denies that the Scripture is without error, which affirms the incarnation but will not affirm the virgin birth, which will affirm the atonement but will not say that Christ died as a sacrifice to satisfy divine justice and reconcile us to God, which will affirm the resurrection but will not say, as our Standards say, that the Lord rose from the dead with the same body in which He suffered, which will say that He wrought mighty works but will not say that He wrought miracles—this is simply one more manifestation of that destructive Modernism which is the deadliest enemy of the Christian religion in practically all of the larger churches of the world at the present day.

Perhaps it will be said that some of the signers of the Affirmation did not understand the full meaning of the document that they were signing, and thought that they were merely objecting to certain things in the procedure of the General Assembly. Well, that may be very comforting with regard to those signers of the Affirmation. But it has not the slightest relevance for the question which we are discussing today. The question which we are discussing today is the fitness of certain gentlemen to discharge the most responsible functions in the Boards of our Church; and it is perfectly clear that such functions, at least, cannot rightly be discharged by gentlemen who, when they signed a formal document like the Auburn Affirmation could not see that the document means what it says.

A mighty conflict is on in the Presbyterian Church at the present time. On one side of the conflict are to be put believers in, and defenders of, the Word of God; on the other side are to be put not only the signers of the Auburn Affirmation themselves, but also all those who are ready to make common cause, without protest, with the signers of the Affirmation in mission boards, in governing boards of theological seminaries, and in the courts and councils of the Church.

The Candidate Secretary a Signer of the Auburn Affirmation.

What has all this to do with the Board of Foreign Missions? It has much to do with it. It may come as a shock to Bible-believing Christians, but it is a fact all the same, that the Candidate Secretary of our Board of Foreign

Missions, Rev. Lindsay S. B. Hadley, is a signer of this destructive document.

The presence of signers of the Auburn Affirmation in any administrative capacity under the boards and agencies of the Church would be disquieting enough. But there is no position where the presence of a person representing such a point of view as that of the Auburn Affirmation is quite so disastrous to the witness of the Church as in the position of Candidate Secretary of the Board of Foreign Missions. To the Candidate Secretary is entrusted the delicate task of interviewing candidates for the foreign field and of encouraging or discouraging them in their high ambition. Is there any agent of the Church who ought to be more completely clear as to what the Church's message is than the occupant of this position? Yet the minister occupying this position has signed a formal document erasing the virgin birth and four other great verities of the Faith from the essential message which the Church is proclaiming in the world.

Serious, however, though the presence of a signer of the Auburn Affirmation in the position of Candidate Secretary is in itself, it is far more serious in what it indicates as to the principles of the Board as a whole. A Board which in the face of criticism, after the issue has been plainly pointed out to it, can retain a signer of the Auburn Affirmation in such a position is an agency which has made its attitude known only too well regarding the great issue between Modernism and indifferentism, on the one hand, and Biblical Christianity on the other. Certainly it is not an agency which deserves the confidence of those members of the Church who adopt the view of Christian missions which is taught in the Word of God.

The Issue Raised by the Auburn Affirmation.

The cancer of the Auburn Affirmation and of what it represents cuts far deeper into our Foreign Board than merely by the presence of a signer of the Affirmation in the position of Candidate Secretary. One of the members of the Board is also a signer of this notable anti-evangelical pronouncement. But the really important thing is that the presence of these gentlemen provides a test to show what the attitude of the Board and of its staff is with regard to the great central issue of the day.

For the staff, Dr. Robert E. Speer, surely, is qualified to give the answer. His answer is given in a letter which, jointly with Dr. John A. Marquis of the Board of National Missions, he sent to me on May 6, 1926:

> "*First*—all the members of the Boards of the Church were elected by the General Assembly. The Assembly clearly believed that they were loyal and faithful ministers and members of the Church. We know of not one who does not accept the Constitution and Standards of the Church and who is not truly and loyally evangelical."

At the time when that letter was written, no less than six out of fourteen ministerial members of the Board of National Missions and five out of fifteen ministerial members of the Board of Foreign Missions were signers of the Auburn Affirmation. Yet all these gentlemen were regarded as "truly and loyally evangelical" by Dr. Speer, and there is not the slightest evidence that his attitude toward signers of the Affirmation has changed since that day.

It must be said very plainly that Bible-believing Christians can have no confidence in a Board whose standards of what is truly and loyally evangelical are such as that. Not even all the eloquence of a man so brilliant, so distinguished and so beloved as Dr. Speer can commend such a Board to them. The only Christ in whom Bible-believing Christians have put their trust is the virgin-born Son of God whom the Scriptures present. And they cannot regard as loyally Christian any mission work in which the full truthfulness of Holy Scripture, the virgin birth, the substitutionary atonement to satisfy divine justice and reconcile us to God, the bodily resurrection and the miracles of our Lord are, all and severally, regarded as non-essential.

IV. MODERNIST PROPAGANDA BY THE CANDI-
DATE DEPARTMENT.

It is not surprising that a Department of our Board which has a signer of the Auburn Affirmation at the head of it should have engaged in Modernist or anti-evangelical propaganda, and as a matter of fact such propaganda has been engaged in by the Candidate Department.

The opportunities for propaganda by that Department are almost unlimited. The secretaries meet the candidates in the most intimate possible way, to advise them about their life work. In their meetings with them, and in their written correspondence, they have the enormous prestige of having been appointed for the purpose by the Presbyterian Church. A young man or young woman says very naturally to himself or to herself: "I am thinking of giving my life to the preaching of the gospel in foreign lands, but before I do so I desire to know what such service involves; the Presbyterian Church which I love and reverance has appointed certain secretaries to tell me; surely I can trust what they say."

How have the Candidate Secretaries used this enormous opportunity of influencing young men and young women? Have they used it for Christianity or for Modernism, for Christ or for Antichrist?

A letter which they sent out on July 15, 1932, may give the answer. That letter was not a private letter. It was signed officially by the Candidate Secretary, Rev. Lindsay S. B. Hadley and by the Assistant Candidate Secretary, Mrs. Charles H. Corbett. It seems, according to its own testimony, to have been sent to over a thousand students and others contemplating foreign service:

"We are sending our greeting in this way to over a thousand of you studying in Colleges, Seminaries, Medical and other Graduate Schools, as well as to some who are getting a year or two of experience before sailing."

This letter does not content itself with advising the students as to their "technical preparation" for a missionary's service. It advises them also about their devotional life:

> "Bible study, prayer, devotional books and some real experience in sharing Christ here will be for your spiritual preparation what your class-room lectures, theses and laboratory work are doing for your technical preparation. A study of the Bible by books or by topics such as 'The Son of God'; 'The Spread of Christianity'; 'The Cross in the Bible' have been found helpful."

That sounds splendid, except for the miserable phrase, "sharing Christ," which so sickens those of us who believe that the work of the missionary or of the Christian at home is not that of sharing an experience but of proclaiming a message.

But what sort of Bible study is here advocated; what is meant by "The Son of God" or "The Cross in the Bible"; what are meant by the devotional books which will be helpful? The letter is not slow to give the answer. It goes on to say, after mentioning the study of the Bible by books or by topics:

> "Then there are books like 'The Devotional Diary' by Oldham; 'Today'; an outline of Bible readings; 'The Meaning of Faith' and others by Fosdick; 'Marks of a World Christian' by Fleming."

What are these books which are here singled out as guides for the devotional life of a thousand young men and young women?

With regard to the books of Dr. Harry Emerson Fosdick, the answer hardly needs to be given to anyone who loves God's Word. Dr. Fosdick is one of the most popular and most destructive Modernists in the whole bounds of the nominally Christian Church. His teachings are diametrically opposed to that great redemptive religion which has hitherto been known as Christianity. He outraged the Presbyterian Church by carrying on his propaganda in the First Church in New York. Then he declined to subscribe to our Standards. Since that time he has continued his Modernist propaganda in the great new church on Riverside Drive.

The only other books recommended (besides the little series called "Today" which is published by our Board of Christian Education) are "The Devotional Diary" by Oldham and "The Marks of a World Christian" by Fleming. These writers are both outstanding Modernists. If any Bible-believing Christian in the Presbyterian Church is still comforting himself by thinking that our Board of Foreign Missions is faithful to its trust, I should just recommend that he examine these two books.

"The Marks of a World Christian," by D. J. Fleming.

The latter of them, *The Marks of a World Christian,* is written by Dr. Daniel Johnson Fleming, a signer of the Auburn Affirmation, who is Professor of Missions in Union Theological Seminary, New York. It is a typically Modernist book, and as one reads it one is impressed anew with the fact that the teaching of Modernism is diametrically opposed to the Christian religion. The root ideas of Modernism are contained in the book, and those root ideas are contradicted by the Word of God.

Dr. Fleming holds that our theology is the explanation of our experience (p. 107); the Word of God plainly teaches that our theology is the truth that God has supernaturally revealed and supernaturally recorded in the Bible: Dr. Fleming holds that God's method is that of incarnation, that although "the most unique and perfect expression of this method was in the Man of Galilee" He is always using the method and indeed "Christianity may be said to be the perpetual incarnation of God in humanity" (pp. 111f.); the Word of God teaches that the incarnation took place once only, when the Second Person of the blessed

Trinity became man and so was and continueth to be, God
and man in two distinct natures and one person forever:
Dr. Fleming holds that "God's greatest gift to us was not
something that he did *for* us but a revealing of himself *to*
us," that "just showing us what he is, and making it possible for us to come into transforming association with him,
will forever be his greatest contribution to mankind"
(p. 112); the Word of God teaches that His greatest gift
to man was something that He did for us when He gave
His only-begotten Son to die for our sins upon the cross:
Dr. Fleming holds that "we are genuinely saved only as
we enter into the experience Jesus had" (p. 113) and that
we "must seek the embodiment of the spirit of Jesus"
(p. 114); the Word of God teaches that we are saved
purely by grace, and that while Jesus was sinless we are
sinful: Dr. Fleming belittles the written Word of God
as compared with the lives of Christians (p. 116); the
Word of God itself offers salvation not through the con-
tagion of Christian personalities but through the gospel
message, and says that all Scripture is given by inspiration
of God: Dr. Fleming belittles correct belief and orthodoxy
(pp. 119, 133, 136, 167); the Word of God says, "But
though we, or an angel from heaven, preach any other
gospel unto you than that which we have preached unto
you, let him be accursed": Dr. Fleming holds the evolutionary or naturalistic view of the Old Testament to the
effect that "even Yahweh, himself, had been honored as
the exclusively national God of Israel" and that it was the
"insight" of the prophets that first led to the view that He
was "the controller of the whole world" (p. 3); the Word
of God says at the very beginning, in a book written far
earlier than the time of the prophets, that Jehovah, the God
of Israel, was Creator of the heaven and the earth: Dr.
Fleming holds (using here the barbarous jargon of modern
religiosity) that "Jesus' faith enabled God to respond to
him in a kingdom way" (p. 78); the Word of God says
that Jesus' work upon this earth was in pursuance of an
eternal plan of redemption: Dr. Fleming holds that "it is

in the cross that we catch such a vision of our God and
his way that ever after life's meaning and possibilities seem
transformed" (p. 80, underlined); the Word of God
teaches that on the cross Jesus paid the just penalty of
our sins in satisfaction of divine justice: Dr. Fleming says
(even underlining at this point his distressing words),
"It is because of this lack of cooperation in us that God is
blocked" (p. 85); the Word of God teaches that He
bringeth all things to pass according to the counsel of His
will.

The examples might be multiplied almost indefinitely,
but what is more important than these details is that Dr.
Fleming's book as a whole is opposed to the Bible as a
whole. It is a different God, a different Christ, a different
way of salvation which is here presented to us; and between the teaching presented in Dr. Fleming's book and
that presented in the Bible there can be no real compromise.
A man may choose one or he may choose the other, but he
cannot possibly choose both.

"The Devotional Diary," by J. H. Oldham.

As for the "Devotional Diary" arranged by Dr. J. H.
Oldham, perhaps its character may sufficiently be indicated
by the paragraph which occurs in the "devotional" readings
for the first day of the first month. It is apparently taken
from J. Middleton Murry, though the method of quotation
is so confused that the reader has some difficulty in dis-
tinguishing the several authors. Here it is:

> "Jesus' teaching is a teaching of life. Life cannot
> be taught, it can only be lived and known. Those
> alone understand the teaching of Jesus who know that
> it is not teaching at all, but simply the living utterance
> of one who had achieved rebirth into a new condition
> of life. Its purpose is to create this new life in others,
> and in those who have ears to hear it new life is
> immediately born."

I ask you, who are members of this Presbytery—even some
of you who have not often agreed with me on the questions

that have come before us in the last ten years—whether you really are willing to proclaim, through your Board of Foreign Missions, a Jesus who "achieved rebirth into a new condition of life," whether you are really willing to acquiesce in this blasphemous attack upon our holy and blessed Lord?

The rest of Dr. Oldham's book is no doubt fairly represented by the quotation which we have just presented. The book is made up of hundreds of quotations, largely from the Modernist writers of the present day—E. F. Scott, John Baillie, Middleton Murry, Hocking, Schweitzer, Harnack, Streeter, etc., etc.—to say nothing of older opponents of the central truth of the Bible such as Seeley and Matthew Arnold; and the most thoroughly destructive of these writers are those who seem to be most frequently quoted. It is such a book which is being commended as *devotional reading,* as *daily food for meditation and prayer,* to the young people who look to Mr. Hadley and Mrs. Corbett for spiritual advice.

Our Responsibility.

Do you really care nothing about it, my friends?

Who is it that is carrying on this propaganda in favor of a Christ who "achieved rebirth"; who is it that is casting despite upon a blessed Name that is above every name? Is it Mr. Hadley alone, or Mrs. Corbett? Is it the Foreign Board alone, which appointed these persons as secretaries?

No, my friends, *you* are carrying on this destructive propaganda if, having the power to stop it, you do not take steps to do so; *I* am carrying it on if, knowing the facts, I keep silent and do not commend this Overture to you today.

Who is it who is being misrepresented by the propaganda of this Candidate Department; who is it whose little ones are thus being led astray by those to whom they look for guidance? Is it one who has no claim upon us, one to whom we may be loyal or not as we please? Oh, no, my friends. It is the One who bought us with His own precious blood; it is He, the Lord of Glory, who calls us now and always to be loyal to Him.

The Way the Books Are Being Commended.

Let it not be said that commendation of a book does not involve agreement with it, and that the recipients of the letter which has been sent by Mr. Hadley and Mrs. Corbett are merely being advised to acquaint themselves, for the enlarging of their minds, with books by the religious leaders of the present day. If that were the manner in which these books are being mentioned, my attitude toward the mentioning of them would be different, though I should still think that the Candidate Department would be obliged to mention with them, and expressly as presenting the Christian versus the Modernist position, books which defend the truthfulness of God's Word. Certainly I am the last to advocate any kind of censorship. I do not believe that Christian people ought to be kept in tutelage. But it is not at all as books which the Christian man should learn to refute that these books of Dr. Fosdick and Dr. Fleming and Dr. Oldham are being mentioned by the Candidate Department. No, they are being mentioned very distinctly as books that are suitable for the nurture of the devotional life. And when they are mentioned in that way, I do deliberately aver that the mention of them constitutes Modernist and thoroughly destructive propaganda on the part of the Candidate Secretaries of our Foreign Board.

Modernist propaganda assails Christian men and women in many subtle and deceptive ways, but never in a way more subtle and more deceptive than in this letter of the Candidate Department of the Board of Foreign Missions of the Presbyterian Church. As I contemplate that propaganda, I think we ought to go down upon our knees to ask God that these young men and young women may be led, by their own reading of God's holy Word, to reject, definitely and forever, the false Christ presented to them by these Candidate Secretaries, through the books of Dr. Fosdick, Dr. Fleming and Dr. Oldham, and may be led, despite this propaganda of an unfaithful Church, to the blessed Saviour presented in the Holy Scriptures, who alone is able to save unto the uttermost those who come unto God through Him.

The Latest Propaganda.

The impression made by that letter of which we have just been speaking is only deepened by the "Spring letter" (also signed officially by Mrs. Corbett and Mr. Hadley) which has just been issued by the Candidate Department. That letter devotes its first page almost exclusively to the book *Re-Thinking Missions.*

What does it say about that book? Does it say that from beginning to end it is written from a radically anti-Christian point of view, the well-known position of modern non-doctrinal religion, which is the deadliest enemy of Christianty all over the world today?

Not at all. It says nothing of the kind. Here is what it does say:

"The Report of the Layman's Inquiry, which is now published under the title, 'Re-Thinking Missions' is the book of the year in Mission thinking and planning. The Commission has challenged many details in the Mission work but their unanimous judgment as to the continuance of mission work is stated as follows:— 'that these missions should go on, with whatever changes, we regard therefore, as beyond serious question.' We are enclosing a copy of Dr. Speer's article 'Re-Thinking Missions Examined' which deals with the critical questions raised by the report. Another leaflet, 'Presbyterian Missions in the Light of Recent Studies' will be published soon, which we will gladly send to any who care to have it and will let us know.

"Certainly two statements at least are of interest to all of you who are thinking of the possibility of mission service. The first is that 'the history of Protestant Missions is a story of the influence of personality upon individuals and communities. The selection and preparation of missionaries is therefore the critical point of the entire enterprise, indeed, it is not too much to say that upon the quality of personnel. far more than upon any other factor, or all other factors.

combined, depends the real and permanent success of the missionary enterprise.'

"Everything depends upon the clarity and thoroughness with which each individual can channel the Spirit of Christ and the love of God both in word and life. It is a tremendous task and we know how many of you are seeking, day by day new insight into His truth and new ways of fellowship with Christ which will make all this possible.

"The second grows out of the first. In addition to the 'power of a vivid personality,' 'spiritual excellence and gentle friendliness of their lives,' the new missionaries should be capable of 'thinking freshly and planning wisely' and meeting with creative minds 'the exacting missionary task of today.' In addition to the thorough professional or technical training and a comprehensive and effective understanding of the Christian message, there should be a 'thorough and impartial study of the history, art and religion of the country, its political, social and economic conditions and the psychology of the people.'

"Here is certainly a challenge to a mighty task and one for which hundreds of you students are preparing with all the earnestness and conviction which the report calls for."

I do not see how anyone can possibly read this letter without getting the impression that the Candidate Department regards the book *Re-Thinking Missions* as being essentially a Christian book, faulty perhaps in detail but reassuring in its main thesis.

That impression is not at all corrected by the reference to Dr. Speer's article. On the contrary, it is only confirmed by that reference; for that reference speaks of Dr. Speer's article merely as dealing with isolated "critical questions" raised by the Report of the Appraisal Commission, and not at all as pointing out the radically anti-Christian thesis which

36

dominates the Report from beginning to end. The point is
not how far that treatment of Dr. Speer's article is fair
to the article. What I am concerned to point out is that
the Candidate Department of our Board of Foreign Missions, in general and also in the way in which it refers to
Dr. Speer's article, speaks of this attack by the Appraisal
Commission upon the heart of Christianity as being essentially a Christian book.

Leading Men Astray.

Even if the treatment of the book *Re-Thinking Missions*
were faulty only in that negative way, it would be bad
enough. The book is one of the religious "best sellers."
It attacks the old, Biblical view of missions, according
to which all mankind are under the awful wrath and curse
of God and may be saved only by an acceptance of the
message of salvation which the Bible presents. It demands a radical change from that view of missions, so
far as the change has not already been wrought on the
mission field. Such a book must be an object of the in-
tensest interest to every young man or young woman who
is thinking of entering missionary service. Surely it is a
book about which guidance is to be expected by such young
men and young women from the Candidate Department of
our Foreign Board, which department undertakes to give
guidance on the most intimate subjects.

What guidance do these young men and young women
obtain? Well, they are told that the book raises some critical questions but is reassuring because it advises the continuance of missionary work.

But that negative fault of the letter of the Candidate
Department is not all. The letter then proceeds to quote
with evidently warm commendation several passages of the
book. They have been reproduced above. As though they
were not bad enough in themselves, the Candidate Department adds a paragraph of its own, which we here reproduce
again :

"Everything depends upon the clarity and thoroughness with which each individual can channel the Spirit of Christ and the love of God both in word and life. It is a tremendous task and we know how many of you are seeking day by day new insight into His truth and new ways of fellowship with Christ which will make all this possible."

This paragraph, with those in which the utterances of *Re-Thinking Missions* are quoted, raises a momentous question. Does everything really depend upon the missionary's personality, or does it depend rather upon the message that he proclaims? The former is the answer of Modernism; the latter is the answer of the Word of God.

When Peter preached the first missionary sermon after he had received the Holy Ghost, he did not do anything that *Re-Thinking Missions* says, and the Candidate Department implies, that he ought to have done; and he did everything that that book says, and the Candidate Department implies, that he ought not to have done. His speech was distressingly doctrinal and distressingly exegetical. He said nothing about his own experience. He did not say: "Look at me, what a wonderful experience I had, how happy I am, how much of the spirit of Jesus I exhibit in my life, how I want to share that experience with you." Instead, he preached, not himself, but the Lord Jesus Christ. He bade men turn away from themselves to Christ. He recounted the external facts regarding Him—His miracles, His death, His resurrection. He spent about half of his time quoting, and discussing in detail the meaning of, the written Word of God. When Paul preached in Thessalonica and elsewhere, it never seemed to have occurred to him to try to save men by the power of his "vivid personality." What he did was to present a message containing a whole system of theology. "Ye turned to God from idols," he says, "to serve the living and true God, and to wait for His Son from heaven, whom He raised from the dead, even Jesus, which delivereth us from the wrath to come."

The truth is that the Bible is opposed to the thesis of *Re-Thinking Missions* and to the implications of the letter of our Candidate Department root and branch. This recent letter, though perhaps not so blatantly offensive to Bible-believing Christians as the one in which they commend as devotional reading the books of Dr. Harry Emerson Fosdick and Dr. D. J. Fleming and Dr. J. H. Oldham, is really just as destructive. The total effect of it is certainly to make the persons to whom it is written look with considerable favor, to say the least, upon one of the most widely read of the anti-Christian books of recent years.

Let it not be said that these are merely details, and that all will be well if these secretaries are cautioned please not to offend the troublesome "Fundamentalists" in the Church by recommending Dr. Harry Emerson Fosdick in the future. No, the real importance of these letters is found in what they disclose as to that which lies beneath. These letters are *symptoms* of a deadly disease. One cannot obtain bitter water from a sweet fountain; and the fountain from which these letters came must be bitter through and through.

But the root of the trouble lies far deeper even than the Candidate Secretaries. Dismissal of the secretaries would not in itself rectify the situation in the slightest. The real trouble lies in the Board that appointed the secretaries and in the General Assembly that elected the Board and in the Church that elected the General Assembly. The Presbyterian Church must decide whether it will stand for Christianity or for Modernism; for the Bible or for the point of view that the book *Re-Thinking Missions* and the books commended by the Candidate Department represent.

V. REFERENCE BLANKS, APPLICATION BLANKS, AND INFORMATION GIVEN TO CANDIDATES.

We have considered the Modernist propaganda which is being carried on by letters issued by the Candidate Department. Very faulty also, from the Biblical point of view, though in somewhat subtler ways, are the questionnaires used by the Candidate Department and the official information given to candidates.

An example is found in the "Candidate Reference Blank," which is sent to persons from whom confidential information is desired regarding prospective missionaries. That reference blank includes among commendable qualities, about the possession of which by the candidate information is desired, such things as "tolerance of point of view of others," "flexibility" (explained as "subordination, when best, of one's own ambitions and preferences"), "desire to progress in spiritual truth," "sanity" (explained as "absence of tendency to extreme views"). Clearly a high mark with respect to those qualities is treated as being in the candidate's favor. No doubt there is a sense in which these questions can be answered in the affirmative even in the case of a man who is most clearly determined to be a real preacher of the gospel. But the trouble is that there are no other questions on this blank to determine whether the candidate is resolved *not* to tolerate, in the sense of holding fellowship with them, those who are opposed to the gospel of Christ as it is set forth in Holy Scripture, and whether he himself is clear in his understanding of the great issue between supernaturalism and naturalism, between evangelical religion and non-doctrinal religion, which now faces the Church at home and abroad. There is, moreover, not one word in this particular blank (though the lack is partially supplied in blanks given to the candidate himself) to determine the candidate's intellectual *attainments* as over against his intellectual *capacity;* there is not one word to determine his knowledge of the contents of the gospel. Such a questionnaire, because of the choice of questions, creates very plainly the impression that "tolerance of opposing views" includes tolerance for views like those of the Candidate Secretary himself and other signers of the Auburn Affirmation, and that such tolerance is far more valued by the Foreign Board than loyalty to the whole Word of God and unswerving opposition to the unbelief that is now so common in our Church.

This impression is not effectively corrected by the various blanks which the candidates themselves are required to fill out. There is, indeed, in those blanks opportunity for the candidate to state what his views are and to give some indication of his intellectual attainments, but there is certainly no clear indication that the Board is concerned to send as missionaries only those candidates who are determined to stand with all their might and main against the Modernism which is the deadliest enemy of the Christian religion at home and abroad.

Among the documents of the Candidate Department is "A Note on the Ordination Vows of the Presbyterian Church." That note contains the following paragraph:

> "1. The question about the Bible should be taken in its entirety. The Church has found during all its years that it can go to the Bible without hesitation or fear to learn its duty *in faith and practice,* finding its norm always in Jesus Christ who is its ultimate authority. The Bible can always be relied upon in these two vital fields and hence it is called 'the only infallible rule' for this purpose. This does not deny the existence of truth in many places; it locates complete reliability in the Word of God."

Certainly this note seems to convey the impression that the spheres of faith and practice embrace something less than the whole content of the Bible, and that the Bible does contain things in other spheres which may not be true. Does that mean that the way is being left open for the shibboleths of modern unbelief to the effect that "the Bible is not a book of science" or "the Bible is not a book of history but a book of religion"—shibboleths which destroy or regard as non-essential the factual basis of our faith, and give over to science the whole realm of facts, reserving to religion only a realm of experiences or of

ideals? At any rate, whether it means that or something
else, it is perfectly clear that Bible-believing Christians cannot agree with it. It is perfectly clear that they cannot
well support a Board which goes out of its way to suggest
to candidates that the Bible is fully true only in two "vital
fields" and may contain errors in other fields.

In many places, the wording of these application blanks
grates upon the ears of Bible-believing Christians, who love
the language of Zion, pleasing though it is to those who
are adepts in the use of the prevailing religious Esperanto.
So, for example, the formal "Application for Missionary
Service" says:

> "I have fully and prayerfully considered the chal-
> lenge and privilege of Christian service abroad and
> desire to share with my fellow-men the inestimable
> values of the Gospel of Jesus."

It is difficult to see how any real missionary of the Cross,
believing that acceptance of the gospel is the only way in
which any man can escape the awful wrath and curse of
God, would desire to speak of missionary service as consist-
ing in "sharing" with his fellow men the inestimable
"values" of the gospel of Jesus.

Taken altogether by itself, that point might not be important. But unfortunately it has to be taken in connection
with the outstanding fact that in modern missionary conferences the very mention of eternal punishment is practically
unheard of, and the motive of fear is regarded as unworthy
and outworn. Yet Jesus, to whose teaching, as distinguished
from the whole Bible, modern missionary leaders are accustomed to appeal, had the most terrible words to say about
the wrath of God and about hell-fire which are found in
the whole of the Bible, and made the motive of fear quite
central in all of His appeal to mankind.

Of course there is more about "sharing" in these blanks.
For example, question 5 in the Application Blank reads:
"What have you in your Christian experience to share with
a group of non-Christians?"; and question 13 reads: "What

values does the church as such bring to you which you would like to share with non-Christians?" I do not think that this objectionable terminology is altogether unimportant. It seems to me that the difference between Modernism and Christianity might almost be expressed by saying that Modernist missionary work consists primarily in sharing an experience, while Christian missionary work consists primarily in proclaiming a message.

Of course we do not get through these application blanks without coming to "the spirit and principles of Christ." That is inevitable. It appears in question 17 in the blank of which we have just been speaking.

Moreover, I sometimes wonder what has become of faith in all of this modern missionary parlance. We hear about persuading men to become disciples of Jesus (question 8 in the "Application for Missionary Service"), but we do not hear anything about faith in the Lord Jesus Christ. Yet faith seems to be rather important in the Bible; indeed the answer which the Bible gives to the question, "What must I do to be saved?" is, "Believe in the Lord Jesus Christ and thou shalt be saved." I do not think that this change of terminology can be waved lightly aside. According to the Bible, a man is not saved by following Christ; he is not saved by loving Christ; he is not saved by surrendering to Christ; but he is saved by faith. And that is an entirely different thing. If he were saved by surrender, or by following Christ, or by love, he would be saved by some high and noble quality or action of his own. But when he is saved by faith, that means that he is saved by God and God alone, and that the means by which God saves him is to work faith in him and lead him, relinquishing all confidence in his own goodness, just to look to the crucified Saviour and say: "Thou hast died in my stead, I accept the gift at Thy hands, O Lord." When a man says that, he is in an entirely different world from the world in which he finds himself in modern missionary conferences, and in modern missionary endeavor. That is the really serious fact which emerges from an examination of the activities of our Mission Board and of most of the other great mission boards at the present time.

With regard to these blanks, we ought never to forget that they will naturally be interpreted in the light of the eloquent testimony as to their meaning which is provided by the presence of a signer of the Auburn Affirmation in the position of Candidate Secretary. Thus the question whether the candidate has "tolerance of point of view of others" will quite naturally be interpreted to mean that he will be expected to be tolerant of a colleague who like the Candidate Secretary regards the virgin birth and four other great verities of the Faith as non-essential. A most important function of a true Candidate Department, on the other hand, would be to see that no candidate should be accepted for foreign service who takes a position regarding the central things of the Christian Faith at all resembling the position which has been taken in a public and formal document by the present Candidate Secretary.

VI. VARIOUS INDICATIONS OF THE ATTITUDE OF THE BOARD, ITS SECRETARIES AND THE AGENCIES WITH WHICH THE BOARD IS CO-OPERATING.

In dealing with the Jerusalem Conference, the Lakeville Conference and the Foreign Missions Conferences of North America, we are saddened most of all, not by the individual Modernist utterances, but by the temper of the whole activity. Judging by the public reports, one could sit day after day in these conferences without hearing anything about the matters regarding which a Christian man should be most deeply interested. We have the feeling, as we read page after page, that if some Bible-believing Christian should stray into one of these conferences and should tell something about the awful wrath and curse of God, about God's retributive justice, which is so prominent in the teaching of Jesus, about the full truthfulness of the Bible, about the death of our Lord as a sacrifice to satisfy divine justice and reconcile us to God, about justification by faith alone, about the utter inability of man to save himself, about the catastrophic return of our Lord, as distinguished from a Kingdom of God which is found only on this earth, about the other world, and heaven and hell—we have a feeling that if some simple, Bible-believing Christian should arise and give utterance to his profound concern about these things, he would seem like some boorish person committing an unpardonable *faux pas* in a fashionable drawing room.

Some people seem to have such a purely negative notion of orthodoxy. They seem to think that a man is orthodox if he merely says nothing outrageous against the Bible and against the gospel of Christ as the Bible sets it forth. What is wrong, people ask, with the preaching of this man or that or with the addresses of this man or that at some missionary conference? Did he say anything that you can lay yours hands on as being directly contrary to the Bible? If not, why do you object to him?

The answer is that there are some of us who think that a preacher of the gospel ought to do something more than avoid saying anything against the gospel; there are some of us who think that he ought to be on fire with the gospel, and that he ought to preach it never so earnestly and never so definitely as in the presence of its opponents, especially when those opponents are proclaiming in the Christian Church another gospel that is no gospel at all.

But in order to preach the gospel with earnestness in that fashion, one must rid himself once for all of the notion that there is any such thing as preaching the gospel positively without preaching it negatively, that there is any such thing as presenting the truth without attacking error. When, at the beginning of the Report of the Lakeville Conference in 1931, a Decennial Conference on Missionary Policies and Method of the Board of Foreign Missions of the Presbyterian Church in the U. S. A., it is said (p. 21) that "the Conference was singularly free from doctrinal clashes" and that "while differences of opinion undoubtedly existed, yet they appeared so small in comparison with the great unity of devotion to our divine Saviour and Lord

and with the urgency of our great commission, that they
found little expression," that indicates with the utmost
clearness that the entire character of the Conference
was quite contrary to the Bible. In that Conference,
Dr. E. Graham Wilson, a signer of the Auburn Affirmation, was a member of the group dealing with evangelism, Mr. James M. Speers, Vice-President of the Board,
commended the Laymen's Foreign Mission Inquiry (pp.
27f.), and it is perfectly evident in other ways that
the underlying differences of opinion struck at the very
roots of the Christian message. Yet the Conference was
"singularly free from doctrinal clashes." Apparently the
members of the Conference thought it to be comparatively
unimportant what the missionary message is to be—in particular, whether it was or was not to be without the great
central verities of the Faith upon which the Auburn Affirmation has cast despite.

A similar impression is conveyed by the report of a
sermon on "A Witnessing Church," by Dr. Lewis S. Mudge,
when (on page 34 of the same volume), Dr. Mudge is reported to have said:

> "Whatever may be your special view of the atone-
> ment, and we are not discussing it to-day in any of
> its technical or theological aspects, it is that which God
> has provided by which God and man may be made
> one."

Here also the deepest things of the Faith, things upon which
the gospel message depends, seem to be regarded as merely
technical or theological.

Moreover, suppose the divergences of doctrinal opinion
at the Lakeville Conference were far less than as a matter
of fact they were—suppose they concerned not the truth
or falsehood of the Bible, but merely the meaning of the
Bible in detail—even then we cannot think that this apparent lack of interest in them is anything other than a
most distressing indication of the sad state of the Church.
The trouble is that the entire centre of men's thoughts in

these conferences is different from that which it would be if the Church were true to the Word of God. I have read many, many pages of these reports, but I can find little in them, I am bound to say, of that profound concern which a Christian man should have for the deep things of the Word of God. Men discuss methods, but that which really matters most of all is simply lost from view.

This general impression, powerful though it is, can never be conveyed by individual citation, and the citations which I shall now make will seem desultory at best. All that I hope to do by them is to make you feel, through their cumulative effect, that there is something sadly wrong with the entire conduct of the missionary work of our Church. But that is not the ultimate aim of what I am trying to say. The ultimate aim is to induce you to take a brave stand, by the help of God, that the Church may not forever go on at this poor dying rate, but may return, with deep repentance for her unbelief and for her indifference to the wonderful things that God has revealed, to a new searching of His holy Word. And when you take that stand, if you do take it, I trust that you may get down upon your knees to ask God to bring us out of this terrible by-path into which we have fallen and back to the true pathway that leads to the City of God.

A. The Lausanne and Jerusalem Conferences.

One of the saddest things in all these recent reports of various conferences in which our Board has been engaged, and in the utterances of Dr. Speer and others, has been the enthusiasm which has been displayed for the vague verbosity of the statement of the Christian message by the Jerusalem Conference. That statement is really a terrible example of what happens when men seek to combine Modernist and Christian interests in the same statement. There is no mention, in clear language, of the things wherein Modernism and Christianity differ; the message is toned down to suit the various interests involved, and the result is sad indeed:

On page 403 of Volume I of the Reports of the Jerusalem Meeting, we have these words, as part of the statement of the Lausanne Conference which the Jerusalem Conference made its own:

" 'The world was prepared for the coming of Christ through the activities of God's Holy Spirit in all humanity, but especially in His revelation as given in the Old Testament; and in the fullness of time the eternal Word of God became incarnate and was made man, Jesus Christ, the Son of God and the Son of man, full of grace and truth.' "

Here we find ignored the distinction between natural revelation given to other peoples and the supernatural revelation given to God's covenant people and recorded in the Old Testament. And when that distinction is ignored, the authority of the Bible is gone. The authority of the Bible is the real foundation upon which Christian missions rest. The true Christian missionary is not the man who says, "This experience has been found to be vital," or the like, but he is the man who opens reverently the sacred volume and says, as he points to its blessed words: "Thus saith the Lord."

It is sad indeed to find Dr. Robert E. Speer saying, in the same volume (pp. 277, 278) immediately after the long contribution of an outstanding Modernist, Dr. Rufus M. Jones, who is reported to be one of the authors of the book *Re-Thinking Missions*—to find Dr. Speer saying, in a chapter on "The Council's Discussion":

"It was felt by all that this subject of the Christian message was the central and crucial theme. There had been differences of view as to whether the method of approach represented in the printed papers had been the wise and true method. And the question had been raised as to whether the missionary forces were united as to the essential and fundamental elements of their message. Was any new and different Gospel proposed?

48

The discussions and the later absolute unanimity of
the Council's action in adopting the report of the Committee on the Message gave a clear and conclusive
answer. The debates, indeed, brought out rich diversi-
ties of thought but not antagonisms. And the final
report represented, truly, a more expansive and comprehensive view than heretofore attained, but also a
positive and unaltered tenacity of loyalty to the everlasting Gospel of our Lord Jesus Christ, the Son of
God."

What sort of union in "the essential and fundamental elements" of the message is it which can unite evangelical
Christians with Dr. Rufus M. Jones?
    At the Foreign Missions·Conference of North America,
1930, Professor Oscar M. Buck of Drew Theological Seminary distinguishes (pp. 144f.) three attitudes of Christians
toward the ethnic religions. The first was the historic attitude of hostility. The second attitude was an attitude of
appreciation of the ethnic religions which very frequently
runs toward syncretism. "I find myself," Professor Buck
says, "very much in sympathy with this attitude of appreciation." Then he presents the third historic attitude in the
following words:

> "The third historic attitude is that of the Jerusalem
> Conference, which to me is an amazing piece of insight
> and expression. Here is a synthesis that gathers to-
> gether all the convictions of the first attitude, and all
> the fair-mindedness and generosities of the second
> attitude, and the point of convergence is the person of
> Jesus the Christ. Jesus Christ is God, speaking to
> us in a Son, greater than all the prophets and all the
> systems, Christianity itself included. These prophets
> of all religions, these systems, only partially represent
> the mind and the life of Christ."

I am very much afraid that Professor Buck's estimate of
the Jerusalem Conference is right. I am very much afraid

that he is right in holding that the Jerusalem Conference, at bottom, represented the difference between Christianity and other religions as being the difference between the superior and the inferior, or at best the perfect and the imperfect, instead of being, as it truly is, the difference between the true and the false.

The real question is, "What must I do to be saved?" The Bible has a very definite answer to that question. Other religions, have different answers. Then the question is whether any of those different answers is right. If any one of them is right, then the answer of the Bible is wrong; for at the very heart of the answer of the Bible is the claim that the Bible's way is the only way.

B. The Board of Foreign Missions on Sherwood Eddy and Kagawa.

In a communication from the staff of the Board of Foreign Missions to the Foreign Missions Committee of the Presbytery of Philadelphia, which was by agreement made a part of the record of the Presbytery, this communication being entitled "Some Brief Comments on the Monsma Report," the following paragraph appears (commenting on page 13, middle, of Mr. Monsma's Report):

> "*Page 13, middle:*—There is no evidence that 'our Presbyterian Board * * * lends official backing' to Dr. Sherwood Eddy and Kagawa; but many worse things could be done than aid Eddy in his virile, student evangelism, and Kagawa in his sacrificial devotion to the doctrine that 'God is Love,' which the 'disciple whom Jesus loved,' thought was orthodox. Eddy and Kagawa are making God and His Christ real and divinely redemptive and vitally reformative to many individuals who become stalwart, fearless and effective followers of their new-found Lord and Saviour."

Bible-believing Christians in the Church have become so accustomed to being shocked by the utterances of ecclesiastical leaders that they are not easily surprised by anything that ecclesiastical leaders may venture upon. But I do think that when they find Sherwood Eddy commended in these warm terms officially by the staff of our Board of Foreign Missions, then they have their breath taken away. Sherwood Eddy is best known, perhaps, for his advocacy of birth control, and for other opinions in the social field. But his lack of sympathy for the way of salvation which the Bible presents is, to say the least, abundantly clear. Some indication of that may be found in what is said in the section below on "Modernism in China." Or take, for example, his book, *Religion and Social Justice*, 1927. Let a man read what he there says about his religious development and then compare that with what the Bible teaches, and I think further argument about Dr. Eddy's position will not be necessary.

Yet the staff of our Board of Foreign Missions thinks that "many worse things could be done than aid Eddy in his virile student evangelism" and that "Eddy and Kagawa are making God and His Christ real and divinely redemptive and vitally reformative to many individuals who become stalwart, fearless and effective followers of their new-found Lord and Saviour." When we read words like that, we are bound to say very plainly that the breach between Bible-believing Christians and the Board of Foreign Missions of the Presbyterian Church in the U. S. A. is profound. Indeed we have the feeling that the staff of the Board in sending a communication like that has indicated that it is so far away from the Biblical position that it has not even the slightest inkling of what the Biblical position is. To such a Board it needs to be said that there are some persons in the Presbyterian Church, despised though they are, who cling to the old gospel with all their hearts as well as with all their minds, and who regard it as an offence against their blessed Lord to support a missionary agency which is in sympathy with the propaganda of Dr. Sherwood Eddy.

With regard to Kagawa, I am bound to say that if I were not already familiar with Dr. Robert E. Speer's willingness to make common cause with men of the most widely diverse attitudes regarding the central thing of the Bible, I should be simply amazed that he should write a commendatory sketch of Dr. Kagawa in preface to Dr. Kagawa's book, *The Religion of Jesus,* as it has been published together with *Love the Law of Life* by the same author by the John C. Winston Company. In Dr. Speer's most recent book, *The Finality of Christ,* he rightly combats, in one passage at least, the error of holding merely to a religion *of* Jesus as distinguished from a religion *about* Jesus; of holding to a mere imitation of Jesus instead of making Him the object of our faith. Yet here he commends in the highest terms, a writer who presents just the view which he there condemns.

On page 56 of Kagawa's book cited above, Kagawa says:

> "Some people will protest that it is an anachronism to-day to speak of the power of redemption. But truly it must be said that anyone who does not believe in a religion of redemption is still very much of a lunatic. Jesus Christ actually experienced it. We find redemptive power in Jesus' experience. This is a sphere which cannot be understood by people who stop short with the religion of Nature."

What possible harmony is there between this redemption which Jesus actually experienced, and which we find because we get redemptive power from Jesus' experience—what possible harmony is there between this redemption and the redemption which, according to the Scriptures, is offered by Christ?

Yet Dr. Speer, who has said some things in rejection of that view, writes a biographical sketch for Kagawa's book, and in his little book, *"Re-Thinking Missions" Examined* he says (page 51) :

52

"The matter [of providing 'effective and adequate Christian literature'] is not primarily one of organization or of finance. It is one of indigenous Christian literary genius. One Kagawa is worth an organization, and his output supports and distributes itself."

C. Dr. John A. Mackay.

It is to be wondered whether those Bible-believing Christians who so lightly pass resolutions expressing confidence in our Board of Foreign Missions are aware of the fact that one of the secretaries of the Board, Dr. John A. Mackay, has published in *The Presbyterian Banner* for January 12, 19 and 26, 1933, a series of articles which gives the most enthusiastic praise to Buchmanism or the so-called "Oxford Group Movement" and to "Barthianism," and clearly presents them both as Christian movements. I cannot enter into an exposition of either of these movements here. With regard to Buchmanism I cannot do better than refer to the admirable pamphlet by Rev. Harold T. Commons;[1] and with regard to Barthianism, to the book reviews by Dr. Cornelius Van Til in *Christianity Today*, for February, 1931, and for December, 1932.

Almost equally disquieting are certain utterances of Dr. Mackay which are reported in the Report of the Lakeville Conference, 1931. For example, Dr. Mackay says (p. 39):

"All Christian activity, and especially all missionary activity, should be regarded as a carrying forward of the Incarnation."

So also he says again (p. 40):

"But in this process of incarnation one thing must continually be borne in mind: the flesh must never cease to be the Word. The new incarnation must not

[1] Harold T. Commons, *Buchmanism*, Price 2 cents. To be obtained from Mr. Commons at 17 South Marion Avenue, Ventnor, New Jersey.

forget to be vocal. Jesus Christ was perfect in word as well as in deed. We must endeavor to be so too."

Then on page 41 Dr. Mackay says:

"The Word became flesh. The Word has become flesh in living men and women. They too must become flesh along the road of the ages, until all flesh becomes a luminous Word and every word an echo of the throbbing heart of God."

D. Dr. Cleland B. McAfee's Report at the Foreign Missions Conference of North America, 1932.

In the Report of the Foreign Missions Conference of North America, which was held at Briarcliff Manor, New York, December 19-22, 1932, the following item, truly amazing to those who think that the secretaries of our Board of Foreign Missions have spoken strongly against the book *Re-Thinking Missions*, appears (pp. 10f.):

"*9. Regarding Laymen's Foreign Missions Inquiry.*—In response to the instructions given at a previous session of the Conference, the Committee on Arrangements, through its Chairman, Dr. C. B. McAfee, presented the following resolution which was seconded by Canon Gould and carried:

" 'The Foreign Missions Conference of North America recognizes gratefully the earnest and unselfish services of the Appraisal Commission of the Laymen's Foreign Missions Inquiry and their constructive proposals. We are at the same time solicitous with reference to unfavorable reactions throughout the Church to the press releases given out in advance of the appearance of the Report, and also to a number of points in the Report itself.

" 'We recommend that in the measures adopted by the boards for fostering the study of the Report, special attention be given to clearing up misunderstandings and to removing wrong impressions, and that we seek to take to heart and profit by the timely and forward-looking recommendations of the Report.

" 'The Conference, in the light of the present most critica¹ World situation, and of the inspiring challenge of thɾ Herrnhut Meeting, as well as of the recognition on the part of the Appraisal Commission of the need of adequate aims and message for the missionary enterprise, wish to reaffirm the Message of the Jerusalem Meeting of the International Missionary Council and the findings of the meetings of the Council at Oxford and Herrnhut dealing with the basis and central emphasis of the world mission in which we are united with the older and younger churches throughout the world.'

"In the discussion on the above resolution, the following took part: Dr. P. W. Koller, Dr. John W. Wood, Dr. Frank Rawlinson, Dr. Alden H. Clark, Dr. W. B. Anderson, Dr. John R. Mott, Dr. A. J. Brown, Miss Grace Lindley, Dr. A. R. Bartholomew, Dr. R. E. Diffendorfer, Dr. Wm. P. Schell, Mrs. Thomas Nicholson, Dr. John A. Mackay, Dr. Robert E. Speer.

"It was moved by Canon Gould, seconded by Dr. John W. Wood, that the Committee of Reference and Counsel be instructed to consult with the Laymen's Foreign Missions Inquiry and the Appraisal Committee and arrange for a conference with them. On motion this resolution was referred to the Business Committee.

"Upon motion of Dr. C. B. McAfee, seconded by Dr. W. E. Lampe, it was voted that the Secretary be instructed to print the action regarding the report of the Laymen's Foreign Missions Inquiry, attaching to it appropriate paragraphs from the Reports of the Oxford, Jerusalem and Herrnhut meetings of the International Missionary Council."

In the light of this resolution, at the passage of which Dr. William P. Schell, Dr. John A. Mackay, Dr. Robert E. Speer, seem clearly to have been present, inasmuch as they are expressly mentioned as having taken part in the discussion, all the opposition which some of these secretaries have expressed to the Report of the Appraisal Commission seems to be rendered utterly meaningless. This resolution of the Foreign Missions Conference carefully refrains from expressing basic disagreement with the Report. The services of the Appraisal Commission are praised, and so are "the timely and forward-looking recommendations of the Report." If Dr. Robert E. Speer, for example, expressed any objection to this favorable treatment of one of the most powerful attacks upon the Christian religion which has been launched in recent years, no record of such objection is found in the Minutes.

I think we discover just at this point one very great objection to what seems to be a widespread policy in our day. What is the time for Christian witnessing; what is the time for clear-cut opposition to anti-Christian propaganda like that of the Report of the Appraisal Commission? We think that such a time is found when a man is in the presence of the enemies of his position. At such time Christian witness-bearing, in its most definite form, is particularly in place.

When Dr. Speer attacks the Appraisal Commission's Report at the Tioga Presbyterian Church in Philadelphia, thereby reassuring Bible-believing Christians in the Church, while at the Foreign Missions Conference of North America he gives every impression of having acquiesced in this resolution, which was actually introduced by his colleague, Dr. McAfee, he is engaging in a course of action with which, to speak plainly, we most strongly disagree. It is not right to encourage Bible-believing Christians to continue giving to a Board whose representatives are not willing to stand up bravely against this broadside of unbelief at a Conference like that at Briarcliff Manor.

E. Dr. A. K. Reischauer on "The Appraisal Commission Report."

In the *Christian Graphic*, Tokyo, Japan, for March, 1933, there appears an article by Dr. A. K. Reischauer, a distinguished missionary under our Board in Japan, on "The Appraisal Commission Report." In it Dr. Reischauer says:

"The Report of the Appraisal Commission will undoubtedly lift the whole foreign missionary enterprise into a place of new significance. Whatever its shortcomings may be, it at least succeeds in forcing the thoughtful reader to 're-think missions.' Whenever an honest re-thinking of missions takes place among real Christians the outcome need not be feared.

"The first newspaper releases, stressing so largely the sensational and adverse aspects of the Report, made a very unfortunate impression in Japan and the Report therefore has to overcome an initial prejudice against it."

As a matter of fact, the newspaper releases were very much more correct in their representation of the Report than is Dr. Reischauer's article or the official statement by our Foreign Board. They were sensational quite properly, because the Report was sensational in its attack upon the Christian religion as the Christian religion has hitherto been known.

Dr. Reischauer says further:

"A few missionaries in Japan accept the Report from cover to cover as 100 per cent correct. They do this, one feels, largely because of the prominence of the Commission's personnel rather than because of what is said. The majority accept large sections, for there is much in the Report which is an old story to missions in Japan. There are many searching passages which cause every conscientious missionary to re-examine himself and his work. The reactions towards such major matters as the missionary motives, the relation of Christianity and the non-Christian religions, etc., have been much the same as in America. Some disagree rather radically with what seems to be the Commission's position, while others interpret the more or less questionable statements in the light of those passages which do seem to conserve what is essential Christianity."

It is perfectly plain that we have here no decision against the fundamental thesis of the Report of the Appraisal Commission; and indeed no such decision, unfortunately, was to be expected from Dr. Reischauer.

F. Dr. Robert E. Speer.

What is the strongest argument among the rank and file of Bible-believing Christians in the Church, who have not followed closely the course of recent ecclesiastical events, against the position which we have been taking regarding the Board of Foreign Missions of the Presbyterian Church in the U. S. A.? I have little hesitation in saying that that strongest argument is found simply in the fact that Dr. Robert E. Speer champions the Board. Hosts of Christian people throughout this country are convinced that whatever Dr. Speer favors must be absolutely sound. They know nothing about the internal workings of the Foreign Board. They know little even about the Report of the Appraisal Commission. They have never looked into the matter of the Auburn Affirmation. They are not aware of the Modernist propaganda which the Candidate Department is carrying on. They do not know that the staff of the Foreign Board has expressed the warmest praise of Sherwood Eddy, the well-known radical teacher. They do not know that Modernism of the most destructive kind is running riot in China and in other parts of the mission field. They only know that Dr. Robert E. Speer endorses the Foreign Board. That is enough for them. They have no desire to look further in the matter; for they trust Dr. Speer.

I am perfectly well aware that when I say that, I am paying a stupendous tribute to the man who is my opponent in this debate. I pay that tribute gladly. I think that Dr. Robert E. Speer is one of the most eloquent men of our time. In my student days, I had that same confidence in his every word which is still had by such hosts of Bible-believing Christians in the Church. In subsequent years I have come to disagree with him with all my mind and with all my heart. I have not come to do so without sorrow, but I have been obliged to do so because of my devotion to what seems to me to be the truth of God. In coming to disagree with Dr. Speer, however, I have never lost my admiration of his brilliant gifts. As I sat and listened to him at the Tioga Church in Philadelphia, when he spoke on the Report of the Appraisal Commission, I said to myself that it was one of the most powerful and brilliant pieces of oratory that I had ever listened to in my life. Physical disabilities, a hoarseness of the voice, which might have destroyed the effect of the speech of any other orator, only seemed to make the more powerful the impression of this speaker's words. I disagreed with the address more strongly than I can possibly tell. Its effect seemed to me to be misleading. It led Bible-believing Christians to put their confidence in a missionary agency which I knew not to be worthy of their confidence. It pleaded for unity between forces between which the Bible teaches us that there can be no possible unity. It cried, "Peace, peace," when there could be no peace. It was mistaken and wrong, and I felt that it was cruel in effect though not in intention. In these days when gifts to foreign missions require genuine sacrifice on the part of devout, Bible-believing Christians, it did seem to me to be very sad that such persons were being led to give to an organization not worthy of their trust. I say that I disagreed with the speech. But I admired the orator, for his oratory, as I have seldom admired any speaker. It is a wonderful thing when such gifts as that are in the possession of a man.

What, then, shall I say of Dr. Speer on the present occasion? No doubt it would be politic for me to say that I agree with his doctrinal teaching, and merely disagree with his policy. By saying that I should be in accord with many persons whom I greatly admire, and who usually support those things with which I agree regarding the policies of the Church. I should avoid arousing prejudice against my proposed overture on the part of those who think that Dr. Speer's teaching is altogether sound. But I am unable to yield to such considerations, where truth is involved. So I am obliged to say frankly that I disagree very seriously, not only with Dr. Speer's policy in the Church but also with his teaching in his books.

I have given expression to that disagreement in my review of his book, *Some Living Issues*, in the October, 1930, number of *Christianity Today*. Dr. Speer will agree with me, I think, that that is a courteous review; he will agree with me, I think, that I have not concealed my high admiration for one whom I hold to be among the most distinguished religious leaders in the world. But at the same time I have given expression to my profound disagreement.

What is the essence of that disagreement? It is found essentially in this—that Dr. Speer is a representative, though the most eloquent representative, of what may be called, for want of a better name, the "middle-of-the-road" tendency with regard to the great issue of the day.

That issue is the issue between Christianity as set forth in the Bible and in the great creeds of the Church and a non-doctrinal or indifferentist Modernism that is represented in the Presbyterian Church in the U. S. A. by the Auburn Affirmation and that is more or less dominant in most of the large Protestant churches of the world.

With regard to that issue, three positions are possible and are actually being taken today. In the first place, one may stand unreservedly for the old Faith and unreservedly against the indifferentist tendency in the modern Church; in the second place, one may stand unreservedly for Modernism and against the old Faith; and in the third place, one may ignore the seriousness of the issue and seek, without bringing it to a head, to preserve the undisturbed control of the present organization in the Church. It is this last attitude that is represented by Dr. Robert E. Speer. He certainly presents himself not as a Modernist but as an adherent of the historic Christian Faith; yet he takes no clear stand in the great issue of the day, but rather adopts an attitude of reassurance and palliation, according high praise and apparently far-reaching agreement to men of very destructive views.

It is this palliative or reassuring attitude which, we are almost inclined to think, constitutes the most serious menace to the life of the Church today; it is in some ways doing more harm than clear-sighted Modernism can do.

The representatives of it are often much farther from the Faith than they themselves know; and they are leading others much farther away than they have been led themselves. Obviously such a tendency in the Church deserves very careful attention from thoughtful men.

But when it is considered, fairness demands that it should be considered as it is presented not by its poorest but by its best exponents. That is the reason why I welcomed so heartily the action of the Presbytery in inviting Dr. Robert E Speer to be present at the meeting of Presbytery when my overture should be considered. His presence would seem to place me at a hopeless disadvantage. He is one of the most eloquent men in all the world; and God has given me no eloquence at all. I have no skill in debate; I have no contagious fire of eloquence. Yet I welcome Dr. Speer's presence. I am convinced of the justice of my cause. I do not want it to triumph merely through any skill of its advocates. If it gains any of your votes today— and it will have to run counter, if it does so, to the entire drift of the times in the world and in the Church—at least this can be said, that it will do so by the sheer weight of truth and justice, and despite an enormous preponderance of superiority which is possessed by the advocate of the other side.

Dr. Speer has been courteous enough to send me, in advance sheets, a copy of his most recent book, *The Finality of Jesus Christ*. It is impossible for me, of course, to express any detailed and reasoned judgment with regard to it. I may do so at some future time, and if I do so I shall do so with all the diligence that I can command. Anything less than such diligence would be dishonoring to an author so distinguished as the author of this book.

But I can say this at least, that this most recent book of Dr. Speer does not change in slightest measure the estimate of his position which I have formed through the reading of earlier books of his and through the reading of his treatment of the Report of the Appraisal Commission in the small book, *"Re-Thinking Missions" Examined*.

In this new book, *The Finality of Jesus Christ*, Dr. Speer says many things, certainly, that are true, many things that are admirably Christian. I wish that I had time to quote them, but it is late at night and this *Argument* must go to press tonight if it is to be in Dr. Speer's hands and in the hands of the Presbytery in time enough to be examined before the meeting.

But despite these admirable features, which appear particularly in the earlier part of the book, I am bound to say that the effect of the book as a whole seems to me to be confusing rather than clarifying at the present juncture in the life of the Church.

The writers whom Dr. Speer most loves to quote are hostile to the Bible and to the Christian way of salvation. It is true that a man may often quote in support of details in his argument the assertions of men who represent a point of view different from his own. But the trouble is that no ordinary reader of Dr. Speer's books would obtain any inkling of the fact that Harnack, for example, whom Dr. Speer loves to quote most of all, represents Jesus as a man who kept His own person out of his gospel and presented Christianity as being essentially an entrance into, and pursuance of, the type of religious life which Jesus Himself lived. The general impression which one gets from the book as a whole is that this writer and the great host of other destructive writers are regarded as valid witnesses to the truth and to the value of the essential Christian message and of the Christian view of Christ. As a matter of fact, if the Christ whom these writers believe to have lived in the first century was the real Christ, then the Christ of the New Testament must of course be given up.

On page 40, Dr. Speer speaks of a modern world view which represents the physical universe as "only a fractional part of total reality," and as "lying ensphered in and operated on by a larger spiritual world." He speaks of that modern world view as though it meant a return to the old view of a transcendent God. We have here what seems to me to be one of the root errors of Dr. Speer's book—the misunderstanding of what the supernatural is. In several places, Dr. Speer seems, as here, to equate the supernatural and the spiritual. There could scarcely be a greater error. By implication it involves a relinquishment of the whole doctrine of a really transcendent God, though I am far from implying that that implication would be accepted by Dr. Speer.

Particularly unfortunate is what Dr. Speer says in Lecture II, which forms the second chapter of the book, about the relation between Christianity and what he calls "Judaism." Nowhere in Dr. Speer's book, so far as I can remember, is there any really clear recognition of the fact that there is really just one religion that is based upon a *supernatural* revelation from God, and that that religion is found in the Old Testament as well as in the New Testament. That is connected with the fact that in this book there is, so far as I have observed, no presentation of any supernatural authority of the Bible as such. There is an authority of "Christ," but no real justice is done to that tremendous view of Scripture upon which our Lord based His own life as a man and which He also inculcated in His followers.

The book, despite some guarding against extremes in this sphere, especially in the early part, is anti-intellectualistic and anti-creedal. Dr. Speer holds that Christianity covered over its original simple message with many involvements, and inevitably thought out the implications of its teaching, and did so of necessity in the thought-forms of those whom it sought to reach. The great creeds are represented as being necessary to guard Christianity's "simple and essential historic centrality." That is rather the Modernist view of a creed than the Christian view, though I do not mean to say that Dr. Speer would work out all its implications. Dr. Speer speaks of the "elaborate verbiage of the creed of the Councils." He speaks of the translation of Christianity into the categories of Hellenistic or other thought as opposed to the "elementary faith." I believe that the implications of all this are very much more serious than Dr. Speer understands them to be.

But, it is impossible for me to treat the book in any adequate way. I can only say again that it seems to me to be essentially in line with what Dr. Speer has hitherto written. My disagreement with his position remains the same as before, and I think I can find in that position the underlying reasons for that policy of compromise in the great issue of the day which has given such profound sorrow to countless admirers of Dr. Speer throughout the world.

In Dr. Speer's book, *"Re-Thinking Missions" Examined,* we find at the end an exhortation to unity. After noting on page 59 that the Report of the Appraisal Commission holds out the intimation that it may be necessary to launch some new agency to carry out the principles of the Report, Dr. Speer says:

"There are already rumors of such an organization. What a tragedy it would be if a movement which

earnestly and fervently seeks for larger unity among
the Churches should issue in a new and rival organization either within or outside of the Churches!"

Then Dr. Speer says further about the same possibility
(p. 60):

"Let one thing, however, be clear. The Churches
and their Boards would go on their way in fidelity
to the New Testament, the historic tradition of the
Christian Church and their Divine Saviour, but they
would not say that any work done by earnest men for
the relief of human suffering and the enlightenment
of human minds and the enrichment of human life
was not justified in appealing for support from those
who were satisfied with the grounds of its appeal."

These passages seem to contradict in the most surprising
way much that Dr. Speer has said in the former part of
the book. If the Report of the Appraisal Commission is
even so bad as it is there said to be—to say nothing of
being so bad as *we* think it to be—surely Christian men
cannot rejoice in the propagation of its errors, whether by
existing organizations or by a new organization. The real
need of the hour, moreover, is not for unity between those
who defend the Report and those who oppose it, but for
separation. Without such separation, we certainly cannot
be true to the Word of God.

If the Board of Foreign Missions tolerates the point of
view of this Appraisal Commission, then it cannot honestly
appeal for support to Bible-believing Christians. If, on
the other hand, it is really true to the Bible, then it cannot
honestly appeal for support to sympathizers with the Commission, but must be willing to bear the reproach of
"intolerance," which is the reproach of Christ.

VII. MODERNISM IN CHINA.

In response to my request by cable, testimony with regard to Modernism in China, in enterprises supported in part or in whole by our Foreign Board, or with which our Board is connected, has been sent to me by Chancellor Arie Kok of the Netherlands Legation in Peiping and by Dr. Albert B. Dodd, Professor in the North China Theological Seminary, who is a missionary of the Presbyterian Church in the U. S. A.

In explanation of this testimony it is to be noted (in the words of Dr. Dodd) "that the Yenching University, the Language School in Peiping, the National Christian Council and the Church of Christ in China, and the Christian Literature Society all get support from our Foreign Mission Board." "The North China American School," Dr. Dodd says further, "is a union school for missionary children in which our Board is financially interested. Quite a number of us have had to send our children to Korea because of the 'modernism' in all the schools provided by our Board in China."

It is to be noted further that the Annual Report of our Board of Foreign Missions includes in the "Union and Cooperative Foreign Missionary Work of the Presbyterian Church U. S. A.," the following (among many other agencies) : Church of Christ in China, National Christian Council (of China), Christian Literature Society (of China), Yenching University, North China Union Language School, Peiping Union Bible Training School for Women, and Shantung Christian University.

The following communication from Dr. Dodd presents reviews of certain books published by the "Christian Literature Society," which, as has just been noted, receives support from our Board of Foreign Missions.

COMMUNICATION from Dr. Albert B. Dodd
A SHORT HISTORY OF CHRISTIANITY
Compiled by A. J. Garnier, 3rd Edition, and Issued by the Christian Literature Society

The author in his preface acknowledges that his work is based on D. C. Somervell's "Short History of Our Religion."

Among a number of other books to which he acknowledges
indebtedness, are H. G. Wells' "Outline of History" and
Hastings' "Encyclopedia of Religion and Ethics."

The author of this work has been set aside by the English
Baptist Mission to give his full time to the Christian Literature Society. This book on church history is a very interesting
text book for middle schools and Bible schools, but in it the
author continually goes out of his way to slander, misrepresent
outstanding contenders and martyrs for the faith, and to
unduly praise "liberals" and other heretics. It is a very
dangerous book, calculated to prejudice the minds of the youth
against those who stand firmly for evangelical truth. The
gnostics are praised as being the first to attempt a philosophic
foundation for Christianity, "though perhaps it is going too
far in their praise to call them the church's earliest theo-
logians as Harnack does." (See page 84.) Celsus is praised
as a skillful and honest opponent of Christianity (page 101).
Of Athanasius, that great hero of the faith, the author says
on page 105, "his name is offensive to very many people because
they have heard it said that he was the author of that overly
strict creed which has been in constant use by the church
through its history. However this creed was not written out
at the time of discussion but made its appearance after his
death and merely bears his name. Nevertheless its ideas and
style are identical with those commonly employed in his
speeches and writings. Athanasius was a bold fighter for the
faith, heroic and strong."

On page 106, he speaks of the creed proposed by Eusebius
at the Council of Nicaea as "an inclusive creed brief and
clear but so brief as to be capable in the opinion of some
scholars of misinterpretations, thus showing the futility of
trying to express theological definitions in words." The result was that this Caesarean Creed was entirely changed by
the Athanasian party, in the Council where it won the
approval of the Emperor, into "a precise but complicated
statement." "The adoption of this creed, however, was not
very fruitful in results."

On pages 111 and 112, the first reason for the persecution
of the early church he gives was its intolerance towards other
religions, looking upon them as of the Devil. "After the
experience of several hundred years, the church has acquired
a tolerant attitude toward other religions, which has gradually
brought it more into accord with the spirit of Jesus and Socrates." The second cause was the doctrine of eternal punishment with which they "terrified the people."

Under the effects on the church of the Roman persecution,
Mr. Garnier devotes eight lines to their edifying effects and
then seventeen lines to showing how those persecutions devel-

oped in the church a most deplorable, revengeful and cruel spirit, quoting at length from Gibbon to prove this point (pages 115–117).

On page 120, Mr. Garnier makes a most absurd comparison between the Nicene Creed and the Sermon on the Mount, of course to the belittling of the former, and then follows this with a statement that "in the fourth century Christians believed more in creeds than in the Gospel." Then on page 121, he goes on to say that, "when Christ preached the Gospel of the Kingdom of Heaven, He did not say that the way into that Kingdom was belief in a creed, but rather that a good personality was required. The very first thing which enabled a follower of Christ to become a true Christian was the use of Jesus' eyesight in looking upon life, and afterwards they obtained the faith of Christ [not faith in Christ. A. B. D.]. Later on Jesus ascended into heaven and men could see Him no more nor receive any instructions from Him. Hence came church organization and with it the necessity of determining the relationship between the new organization and its foundation, Christ Jesus, and the further necessity of clearly defining the mutual relationship between Christ and God. But it is very difficult to arrive at the solution of this question. More and more Christians employed their mental powers on this question. Gradually the discussion centered on belief as to facts concerning Jesus, as they regarded this as the most important matter, and they used this as the measure of a Christian's qualifications. But if we but look at the four Gospels we may clearly see that this is not the most important matter. It is rather to examine our hearts and see whether we can keep there the same faith which Jesus had."

On page 190, Abelard is spoken of very highly as a progressive, and Bernard just as slightingly as a narrow conservative.

On page 234, the author is fulsome in his praise of Erasmus and his pacific policy toward the Papacy in contrast to the revolutionary one of Luther, and states that his contribution to the progress of the church was greater than Luther's. He is altogether too harsh in his criticism of Luther's weak points and most bitter and unjust in what he says of Luther's connection with the Peasant War.

Chapter XIX is entitled "The Modern Current of Thought in the Christian Church." In it he holds the doctrine of the infallibility of the Scriptures up to ridicule as a doctrine held by the church sixty years ago and still clung to by not a few Christians, but which he takes for granted is contrary to the findings of science. He describes a battle line that is being drawn by Fundamentalists and Modernists over such doctrines as the virgin birth, the bodily resurrection of Christ, the verbal

accuracy of the Scriptures, the substitutionary theory of the
Atonement, and the miracles, and then concludes that there
is room for both types of thought in the church and that
there is no need to quarrel over such matters, for what Christ
emphasized was simply "following Him and loving one's
neighbor as oneself."

Altogether I consider this a very dangerous book and I
deplore its use in so many of our mission schools.

FUNDAMENTALS OF THE CHRISTIAN RELIGION

OUTLINES FOR GROUP STUDY, ARRANGED BY T. R. GLOVER
PREPARED IN CHINESE BY M. T. LIEN, EVAN MORGAN
CHRISTIAN LITERATURE SOCIETY, 1932

This book contains the following teachings on the Atonement:

It attacks the substitutionary doctrine of the Atonement.
It says the Old Testament doctrine of the sin offering was
inconsistent with the justice of God, holding that God coveted
bribes, citing Psalm 50:12 in this connection. It states that
the New Testament while making use of the figures drawn from
Old Testament sacrifice, attached no importance to the ceremonial ordinances. The wrath of God could not as before be
appeased in this way. Sin was each man's own debt and could
not be borne by another, still less could it be borne by a sacrifice, Hebrews 10:1–4. Christ's Atonement was totally different from those sacrifices. Christ was sent to show God's
love, and the climax of His love was in dying for mankind;
hence His death also may be viewed as a sacrifice. [His]
reformed teaching was to lead men to know the truth and
thus obtain liberty, John 8:32. He sacrificed Himself in
winning a victory for the truth (pages 37–38).

The [New Testament] statements about His redeeming from
sin through the ransom price of His blood and about cleansing
and washing away sin by His blood, are altogether the figures
of poets, the imaginations of literary men. They are not at
all statements of facts (page 38).

"To say that Christ's blood means His death and that
on account of that death God draws near to men does
violence to human reason." (Page 38.) "If an earnest
patriot by sacrificing his life to save his country there-

by inspires the entire body of his fellow countrymen to a determined stand against the enemy and thus the country is saved, it is not that He can redeem his country by his blood, still poets may sing of this deed, 'Hot blood flows a thousand ch'u, to cleanse ten thousand li of shame' . . . . So Jesus could not become a sacrificial offering . . . . His death was His will—His choice, Hebrews 10:10. By His will He was able to show forth the fundamental nature of God, and more especially His love. We may know that the real nature of God is indeed love. God through the death of Jesus reconciled us to Them [probably means to God and Christ] . . . . Hence when we think of the death of Jesus, a thousand times ten thousand times [I exhort you] do not think that Jesus was an offering of sacrifice."

From lack of time I confine myself to this one part of this terribly dangerous textbook.

BRIEFER NOTES ON VARIOUS BOOKS.

"The Prophets of Israel from the Beginning of the Assyrian Period to the Time of the Maccabean Wars," by L. Gordon Phillips, translated by Chuan Shuang Ken.

This book is a theological text-book used in a union Theological Seminary in Amoy and doubtless elsewhere. It is thoroughly "modernistic" and destructive of faith in the Word of God as one might infer it would be by the special acknowledgment on the part of the author to Hastings' Bible Dictionary and C. F. Kent's teaching on page 6.

On page 5, he says that Amos, Hosea, Nahum, Zephaniah, Jeremiah, Obadiah, Malachi, Joel and Jonah were added to by later writers who wanted to add a message for their own times, and that Isaiah, Micah, Habbakuk, Zechariah were the composite works of quite a number of authors and redactors. He proposes in this book to separate them into their various parts and arrange each section in its historical order.

On page 12, he says Is. 24–27 and Zech. 9–14 obtained the place they occupy by their authors falsely using the names of the earlier prophets Isaiah and Zechariah. The author of Daniel, taking the name of a prophet who left no other book, could not get his work into the second volume of Hebrew Scripture which was already closed to new works.

The Book of Isaiah is an intricate conglomeration, according to this author, whose composition extended from the time of the real Isaiah until the 2nd century B. C. (page 39).

(Page 114) Zechariah uttered his prophecies in the form of visions as a clever method of attaining his object without exciting the suspicions of the Persian Government. [In other words he falsified in calling them visions.] Obadiah was not a man of as broad a vision as the Second Isaiah. In his opinion [such expressions as this are continually used by the author] the calamity which overtook Edom was God's punishment for their enmity against Judah . . . , hence the thought of Obadiah was not much above the level of the ordinary citizen" (page 132).

"Malachi laid too much stress on the outward forms of God's worship." (Page 134.)

"There are many evidences which prove the book of Jonah to have been written about the year B. C. 300. (Such as his Aramaic words, his universalism and his quotations from Joel.)" (Page 154.)

"The book [Jonah] is allegorical like the Parables of Jesus and Pilgrim's Progress. It was originally intended to be a story book and not history." (Page 155.)

The book of Daniel, the author says, was written in the Maccabean period to inspire the faithful Jews by relating stories of ancient citizens who in spite of persecutions faithfully served God and preserved a firm faith in Jehovah and boldly witnessed that He alone was to be worshipped, etc., etc. (page 160).

Zech. 9–14 though written about the same time as Daniel (about 160 B. C.) by an anonymous writer, was "much more fortunate than the book of Daniel in that, through being appended to the book of the prophet, Zechariah, it obtained a place in the Book of the Prophets." At this time prophecy had fallen to its lowest level . . . . He was most patriotic but also exceedingly narrow, dwelling minutely upon the terrible fate of the Gentiles . . . ." "Estimated from the standpoint of religious and ethical value these chapters in the Old Testament are of not much account and are of the same class with Esther, a book brought forth out of the same period." (Pages 161–162.)

In the closing paragraph of the book, the author says, "Some of these prophets were only a very little above the spiritual level of the people as a whole, all others of them could do was to fan into flame the feelings and hopes of the people, still others really heard the voice of God, understood His will and stood out above the general level of the people . . . . These (of the last class) like John the Baptist prepared the way for Jesus, and they performed the function of prophets not because of their prophecies but because of what they were themselves."

A book entitled "Prayers" by Professor T. C. Chao of Yenching Theological College, Peking, a School in which our Board is interested, was issued by the Christian Literature Society, Shanghai, in 1931.

This book is dedicated to "My Teacher and Friend Wilbur Fisk Tillett, D.D., S.T.D., LL.D., Dean Emeritus, School of Religion, Vanderbilt University."

Professor Chao is a well-known "Modernist," and he shows this in his little book of "Prayers." There are 42 prayers in the volume and I have failed to find in any of them any reliance placed on the Atonement as a ground of forgiveness of sins. His second prayer is an evening prayer and quite properly abounds in confession of sin and he repeats the thought, "We would repent with sorrow and beseech Thee to forgive us," as if such repentance were all that was necessary. Not even the special prayer for Good Friday reveals the least sense of having been ransomed by Christ's precious blood.

A book of Sherwood Eddy's on "Sex and Youth" has been translated into Chinese by some other society but I notice its sale is promoted, in connection with a household library, both by the C. L. S. and the Church of Christ in China.

Other noted "Modernists" whose works are published by the C. L. S. are Fosdick and Kagawa. A recent book of the latter so published is on the religious education of children. As usual in his books he therein freely expresses his convictions that the Old Testament has a large legendary element which is therefore historically untrustworthy. He says if he had five hours for the religious education of children he would not spend more than one of them on the Bible.

The Biblical Basis of Christian Ethics, by Prof. Lyman V. Cady, B.A., S.T.M., with the collaboration of Rev. C. Y.

Gwoh, B.A., S.T.M., of the Cheloo School of Theology, Tsinan (a union school supported by the English Baptist, American and N. Presbyterian Foreign Mission Boards. etc.), published by the C. L. S., Shanghai.

This is a thoroughly rationalistic book. On page 9, he states that the creative work of the prophets (dating from the eighth century on as he later shows) was the beginning of Hebrew religion.

On page 12, he claims that the prophets from their religious experience came to see that God's nature was an ethical one.

(Page 11) "Seeing with their own eyes society everywhere filled with unrighteousness and darkness, they could not but cry out vehemently and with outstretched arms," predictions of speedy and certain retribution.

(Page 12) "The thought of individual relationship to God did not arise until the time of Jeremiah and Ezekiel."

(Page 13) "The prophets all felt that . . . was something Yahveh abominated. The book abounds with statements of what the prophets or N. T. writers or Jesus "felt" or "thought" or "supposed," in true destructive higher critical style.

(Page 17) In the midst of the exile there arose an anonymous "great thinker" to whom we are indebted for Is. 40–66. He represented the sufferings of God's servant Israel as possessing redemptive power for the gentiles; after many years, Jesus applied this figure to himself.

(Page 19) "We may know that the religious and ethical thought of the prophets was the first layer of the foundation upon which the personality and teaching of Jesus was built, and by the use of historical eyesight may see that without these prophets who preceded him, the personality and teachings of Jesus certainly could not have been developed as they were."

(Page 21) "While Jesus accepted every correct reasoning and teaching of the ancient prophets, he continually remoulded the thoughts of his predecessors upon the basis of his feeling and experience of God."

"The views of Jesus as to God and man were a step in advance of the prophets." Of the Book of the Covenant, Ex. 20:22–23:33 which, he claims, was written in the wilderness or soon after the arrival in Canaan, and was thus the earliest portion of the Torah, he says that its religious ordinances were especially senile and without much ethical value, and that in his opinion "this law-code is merely a conglomeration of legal decisions, religious ceremonies and primitive 'taboos.' "

(Pages 24–25) Deuteronomy, of course Mr. Cady holds, was written in the time of Jeremiah with the object of realizing the prophetic hopes in regard to justice and right human relationships, and for this reason much was added to the ancient code of laws, ascribed by tradition to Moses, upon which the book was based. While there is much in the book of an elevating nature for the contemporary social life and thought of Israel, "it is a pity that they did not extend those lofty ideas to their enemy nations but still supposed that Jehovah's command was to destroy all alien enemies. The rule of justice contained in this book is still that of revenge, only somewhat milder than it was at first."

(Page 26) He teaches that the Priestly document was written 572–444 B. C. by priests who put the laws they had received from tradition into writing. This class of priests later pieced together what is now our Hexateuch, and in doing so altered the historical records, ceremonies and laws in accordance with their preconceived notions. "It is a pity that the Priest Code looked upon ceremonial cleanness and regulations in the same way as ethical virtues of the inner life, supposing that the command of God was the source of all these obligations."

In Chapter Four, "Jesus and the Apocalyptic Teaching," the apocalyptic writers, among whom the authors of Daniel and Revelation are explicitly included, are described as "enthusiastic dreamers" who "thought out a new method" by which God would save men from the present evil age (pages 38–39). In this, they were influenced by the Persian dualism (pages 41–42). As to the effect of this mode of thought upon Jesus he presents three views as held by modern men:

(1) Its conceptions controlled Jesus' thought as to his own mission and influenced all his thinking.

(2) Jesus accommodated his teachings to his disciples who held these conceptions.

(3) Jesus was himself entirely free from this influence. After dismissing with a bare statement the *older* form of this view, based mainly upon the ground of Preexistence (of Christ), that He had a sure insight into the future and saw that the Kingdom of God among men, having character at its very center, could not come suddenly in a miraculous supernatural manner, he discusses at length and in a very commendatory way the *modern* form in which it is being advocated upon the basis of the most minute critical study of the New Testament through which the attempt is to show that the disciples failed to give the real non-apocalyptic teachings of Jesus but distorted them by their own preconceived ideas. Mr. Cady thinks either (2) or (3) correct (pages 43–50).

On page 59, he speaks of "the experience Jesus had of God
as man's father and the conception he had of sonship to God
being the making of the Heavenly Father's will and work His
own will and work" as "the source of this high and wonderful
view of human life," and that "this creative talent arose from
Jesus' religious life." "We may take this as a philosophic
principle and hold that a religious faith like that of Jesus . . .
truly contains within itself exceedingly great power."

On page 61, "Jesus felt that other men all had a part with
him in this fundamental relationship of union with God."
(The immediate context shows that this relationship was that
of being God's son.)

"Jesus from His experience recognized that sonship was
an individual moral idea."

On page 63. "The consciousness that he was God's son was
the source of the deepest power within Jesus' nature."

On page 71. "The moral interpretation of Jesus' casting
out devils was his freeing men from fear."

On pages 71 and 72, we have the author's analysis of the
meaning of "God's Son" as exhibited in Jesus' own person.

The five points he gives all exhibit the relationship merely
as a moral or psychological one which can be shared with
other men, and he concludes this subject with a quotation from
E. W. Lyman: "Jesus' conception of the 'Son of God' gives
us an idea. It makes us sure that the spirit of every man is
of infinite worth. Moreover because Jesus made actual use
of this conception, all kinds of forces have been started which
may enable every man to arrive at that actual estate which is
above all price."

In his discussion of the writings of Paul and John the author
discounts all that they said which would put any deeper content into the relationship of Jesus to God. I can find nothing
in the entire book that would lead one to think that Mr. Cady
believes in the deity of our Lord, or in His substitutionary
atonement; which bears out the common report of students
and missionaries that he is a unitarian.

In a translation of Dr. Stanley Jones' "Christ of Every
Road," by M. T. Lien and Evan Morgan, published by the
C. L. S. in 1932, the sense of the paragraph from page 56 of the
original, "And think how men misconceived God even in the
history of Israel, where the highest conception of God was
found among men. A mother was explaining to her little girl
about the murder of the Amalekites. She said that revelation

was progressive, and that now in Jesus we were told to love our enemies and to do good to them that despitefully use us. The little girl thought a moment and then her face lighted up and she said, 'Now I understand . . . this back here was before God was a Christian'" is changed to read "This mistaken conception of God was not only entertained by the gentiles, but could not be avoided even by the Israelites. A mother was telling her daughter the story of the murder of the Amalekites by the Israelites. Her daughter remarked, 'God is love. He could not have approved of the murderous deed of the Israelites, because Jesus has manifested God's nature. Since God is love, He loves not only His neighbors but also His enemies.' From this girl's reply we may know her background. The true God was at its center, hence her true insight here expressed" (pages 29–30).

On page 55, the "B. C. God" is spoken of disparagingly in contrast to the "A. D. God."

B. COMMUNICATION FROM CHANCELLOR ARIE KOK.

MEMORANDUM
concerning
MODERNISM IN MISSIONS
under the
NORTHERN PRESBYTERIAN FOREIGN BOARD
(more particularly in North China).

1. MODERNIST CANDIDATES FOR THE FOREIGN FIELD ARE BEING ACCEPTED BY THE NORTHERN PRESBYTERIAN FOREIGN BOARD, AND SENT OUT ON THE SAME FOOTING AS CONSERVATIVE CANDIDATES.

More than twenty years of close observation in different parts of China have established the fact beyond any shadow of doubt that all types of Presbyterian missionaries ranging from strong conservatives to rank modernists have arrived on the field, being accepted and sent out by the Board. The influx of modernist Presbyterian missionaries is at present less than six or seven years ago, when their number was

COMMUNICATION FROM CHANCELLOR ARIE KOK.

alarmingly great. The conservatives are still in the majority. The presence, however, of militant modernists working in their midst as colleagues or occupying strategic positions, has a marked effect on the conservatives themselves. Many of them have become religious pacifists, who desire peace at any price and have surrendered to modernist leadership.[1] The fact that they are regularly attending the so-called Union Churches, where, as in the case of Peiping, the Pastor is a modernist, the pulpit is time after time occupied by outstanding modernists, and the publications of the University of Chicago are being used as text books proves their surrender. Those amongst them, who have remained loyal in their stand for the Scriptures and for Presbyterian standards, find themselves often more hampered in their contention for the faith by the pacifist attitude of their conservative brethren than by the activities of their modernist colleagues.

Both conservatives and modernists enjoy the same standing and they labour in the Chinese Churches on an equal footing. The rank modernist has as much right and liberty to propagate his views from the pulpit and in classes as the loyal evangelical. As both types of missionaries are usually working side by side in the same station, conflicts often arise, causing confusion in the Chinese mind and definitively hampering constructive work. It must be remembered that the conservatives were first in the field, the modernists were sent out later. The latter break down what the former have been trying to build up whilst loyal conservatives feel bound by their conscience to counteract the destructive influ-

---

[1] My terminology differs at this point somewhat from that of Chancellor Kok. I should be inclined to say that "religious pacifists, who desire peace at any price and have surrendered to Modernist leadership," are to all intents and purposes not only Modernists but the worst kind of Modernists. (J. G. M.)

ences of their modernist Colleagues. In many cases the situation has become impossible, resulting either in the conservatives grouping together for unhampered constructive work (North China Theological Seminary, Tenghsien) or in the conservatives being induced to compromise (Peiping Station), thereby paving the way for a peaceful, but not less sure penetration of the modernist leaven in their churches.

This impossible situation could have been avoided if the Board had refrained from sending out modernist missionaries in the fields, already occupied by conservatives. By accepting modernist candidates and supporting modernist missionaries on the field, the Board cannot escape their share in the responsibility for the penetration of modernism in the missionary body and in the churches.

Some names of modernist Presbyterian missionaries, stationed at Peiping, appear on the inside cover of the magazine "Life and Truth," Vol. III, No. 4, January 1933, a publication of the Yenching University. At least seven other names must be added to make the list of modernist Northern Presbyterians in Peiping complete. As the Directory of Protestant Missions in China, 1932 edition contains 30 names of N. P. missionaries, the modernists and conservatives in Peiping are about equally strong.

2. YOUNG MISSIONARIES—BOTH EVANGELICALS AND MODERNISTS—ARE REQUIRED TO SPEND THEIR FIRST YEAR ON THE MISSION FIELD IN THE DEADENING ATMOSPHERE OF A SCHOOL WHICH IS UNDER MODERNISTIC DOMINATION.

This School is the North China Union Language School, now called "College of Chinese Studies." From the very start the Presbyterians extended "financial and other cooperation" to the School.

COMMUNICATION FROM CHANCELLOR ARIE KOK.

For more than 14 years, Mr. W. B. Pettus, a former Y. M. C. A. worker, a rank modernist, . . . is the Director of the School. Whilst the main object of the school is the study of the Chinese Language, yet, the lectures, services, discussion-groups and socials (dancing in the School is permitted) are distinctly leading away from the evangelical faith and from an undivided devotion to the task of a missionary. The students reside in the School hostel and the Director considers it his duty to exercise his influence in such a way as to keep the students away from anything that is definitely evangelical and encourages the young missionaries to join in with modernist groups, Union Church, etc. Many a young missionary has lost his first zeal, his love and his missionary enthusiasm in the Language School and not a few weak characters have been led away from the evangelical faith under the influences of the School. For these reasons several missions, as for instance the Baptist Mission, the Free Methodist Mission, the Foreign Missions in Many Lands, etc., have voted against sending their missionaries to the Language School.

The Northern Presbyterian Board by giving its consent to cooperate with the North China Union Language School, by supporting it at least for a period of ten years, and by placing their young unexperienced missionaries for their first year under the leadership of a modernist Principal, cannot escape their share in the responsibility for the spiritual and social shipwrecks which were made in that School.

3. THE RIGHT OF MODERNIST MISSIONARIES TO PREACH AND PROPAGATE MODERNISM IN THE CHINESE CHURCHES IS RECOGNIZED.

This is self-evident, as it is only a reflection of the situation in the home-churches. But it is far more serious in the mission field, where the young Chinese Christians do not

COMMUNICATION FROM CHANCELLOR ARIE KOK.

possess that historical background, Christian experience and spiritual ancestry which is the backbone of the churches in the West. Being unexperienced and unable to discern, they are an easy prey to modernism with its syncretistic religious background, and, once started on the path of denial, they do not know where to halt and often fall back in gross unbelief and atheism.

The Board by encouraging the application on the field of the so-called "inclusive policy," has assisted in opening the dyke to the floods of doubt and unbelief, thereby causing inestimable damage to the native churches. The majority of the Chinese modernist leaders in their denial of revealed truth have already gone far beyond the line drawn by their foreign teachers, who are themselves becoming more and more alarmed about the eagerness of their pupils to throw away everything.

The "inclusive policy" in the home churches constitutes a real danger; on the field it is a formidable disaster and the Board cannot escape their share in the responsibility for the deplorable results caused by favoring the "inclusive policy."

4. PRESBYTERIAN MISSION FUNDS ARE BEING USED FOR THE SUPPORT OF ORGANIZATIONS WHICH ARE DOMINATED BY MODERNISTS AND WHICH AIM AT A UNION OF ALL DENOMINATIONS INTO ONE BIG LIBERAL CHINESE CHURCH.

In China these organizations are:

a. The National Christian Council of China.
b. The Church of Christ in China.

As their aims are widely known at home, there is no need for going into detailed statements. The best evidence that these bodies are indeed aiming at a swinging around of all Churches to the modernist camp, is the fact, that ap-

COMMUNICATION FROM CHANCELLOR ARIE KOK.

proximately 2000 missionaries in China and 75,000 Chinese
Christians have understood it to be so and now definitely
refuse to be tied up with these bodies, the evangelical missionaries being federated in the "Bible Union of China"
and the evangelical churches in the "League of (Evangelical)
Christian Churches."

As a specimen of the type of men, which were chosen
to serve as official full-time secretaries of the National
Christian Council an extract of an article is attached hereto,
written by Dr. H. T. Hodgkin in the Official Organ of the
N. C. C.

THE BULLETIN

OF THE

NATIONAL CHRISTIAN COUNCIL

No. 14.   Published at 23 Yuen Ming Yuen Road, Shanghai.   Apr., 1925.

LEADERSHIP

One is your Leader, even Christ . . . . All ye are
brethren.   Matt. xxiii:10, 8.   He gave some to be apostles.
Eph. iv:2.

A great man has fallen.   In the death of Dr. Sun Yat
Sen China has lost the one outstanding figure in her
public life.   We may dislike his policies or criticise his
methods, but this man, above all contemporary Chinese,
had the power to kindle enthusiasm and to win devotion.
Others may have been cleverer, more far-seeing, more
prudent.   Dr. Sun was *par excellence* a leader of men.
In this day when there is so urgent a need for leadership
it may be well to ask what were the qualities which
marked out this man for such a position.

* * * * * *

COMMUNICATION FROM CHANCELLOR ARIE KOK.

Our generation has seen another leader of men who had many similar qualities. In Lenin we see a man possessed by an idea, with courage and self-sacrifice, a lover of the people.

* * * * * *

. . . The characteristics seen in these leaders are among those we value most highly in the personality of Jesus Christ. In self-forgetful devotion, in courage, in sympathy with no shade of patronage, He stands supreme.

. . . The Christian fellowship calls for leadership of a different kind. The Captain of our Salvation was in our midst as a Servant—"the first among many brethren."

The problem of leadership, then, is suggested by the two verses with which we began. We need those who will be real leaders, with qualities which mark them out for apostleship. Devoted and fearless they must be, people with larger vision and stronger faith than the average. Yet these qualities must make no barriers between the leaders and the rank and file. Leaders and followers alike are part of one family . . . .

* * * * * *

H. T. H.

As a specimen of the type of men that are prominent in the Church of Christ in China, an article in Chinese is attached hereto[1] by Dr. Cheng Ching Yi, First Moderator of that Church, in which he denies the bodily resurrection of Christ, as pointed out in an article by the Editor of the "Spiritual Food Quarterly," Mr. Wang Ming Tao; as a specimen of the type of men that are being welcomed by these bodies and given opportunities to carry on their insidious propaganda within the churches, an article is attached hereto written by Mr. A. Kok, in regard to the latest campaign in China of Dr. Sherwood Eddy, a well known modernist, socialist, advocate of birth control and Soviet sympathizer.

(1) Not printed here, since translation is not immediately available.

COMMUNICATION FROM CHANCELLOR ARIE KOK.

(Reprint from the January-March 1932 issue of "The China Fundamentalist," published by the Christian Fundamentals League for China, Shanghai.)

DR. EDDY'S CAMPAIGN AND ITS IMPLICATIONS

A. Kok.

Dr. Sherwood Eddy can be satisfied with his recent "evangelistic" campaign in China. From his viewpoint it was a considerable success.

The Y. M. C. A. platforms everywhere were, of course, open to him, because he came "at the invitation of the National Committee of the Y. M. C. A." [1] and all "the arrangements for his program were in the hands" of that Committee. [2] Representatives of other national organizations, in particular the National Christian Council of China, have been cooperating whole-heartedly. Several large local Chinese Churches have opened their doors for him, whilst some Western Churches whose membership is made up for the greater part of modernist missionaries, as for instance the Peking Union Church, have invited him in their pulpit. [3] It goes without saying that liberal missionary institutions of the Yenching University type were most eager to have him address their student body.

More than twenty large educational centers all over China were reached and "multitudes of students and other young men and women of the educated classes have heard him wherever he has gone." [4] The campaign was one of the largest of its kind undertaken for some years. It lasted for five months. Dr. Eddy's messages are reported to have received "a remarkable response" [5] and the work is now being carefully "followed up" by like-minded Chinese leaders and foreign missionaries in various cities of this country.

The mere fact that a campaign amongst Christian constituencies under leadership of a man like Dr. Eddy has been possible is in itself a most significant sign of the times and affords fresh proof of the alarming degree in which

---

[1] "The Bulletin of the N. C. C.," No. 37, June 1931.
[2] "The Bulletin of the N. C. C.," No. 38, Dec. 14, 1931.
[3] "The Leader," Oct. 23, 1931.
[4] "The Bulletin of the N. C.," No. 38, Dec. 14, 1931.
[5] Ibid.

COMMUNICATION FROM CHANCELLOR ARIE KOK.

modernism in its various ramifications is rapidly gaining ground on the mission field.

Who is Dr. Eddy? He is best known as a Y. M. C. A. man. For several years he worked in India as National Secretary of the Y. M. C. A. until 1911, when he was appointed Secretary for Asia work of the International Committee of this Association labouring among students of Japan, Korea, China and India. In his China campaigns he closely collaborated with Dr. John R. Mott. In those days already his radical views greatly alarmed Christian leaders in the U. S. and elsewhere, the general feeling amongst them being expressed in these few words: "Mr. Eddy is a sample of the leadership that is now wrecking the faith of hundreds of our young men and women."(⁶)

Since 1922, Dr. Eddy has paid repeated visits to Soviet Russia and was particularly welcomed in Moscow during the year 1926, when he headed a group of "pink" Y. M. C. A. workers and others. It is only quite recently (1931) that he resigned from his position in the Y. M. C. A. On that occasion it was reported: "Sherwood Eddy, who has been using the Y. M. C. A. as a cloak for his pacifistic, socialistic, internationalistic, pro-Soviet activities, has at last shed the cloak and emerged in true or almost true character."(⁷)

From the great mass of material which throws light on Dr. Eddy's present religious and other views, it is only possible to select a few of the most striking passages:

' "Too long has the Bible been set up as a text book of law, science and everything else, and Christians have paid a bitter price for trying to keep it as such," declared Sherwood Eddy . . . to three thousand students and others meeting at . . . Church. "There has been a conspiracy of silence," he declared. "If you try to make that book infallible in all matters the world is doomed. I won't have thousands of young people lose their faith because it is demanded that they accept some antiquated dogma derived from it. . . . Such controversial matters as the

---

(⁶) "Biblical Recorder," Dec. 1, 1925, quoting from "King's Business."

(⁷) "Items of Interest," No. 6, Feb. 10, 1931. Cf. "Pastors, Politicians, Pacifists," by LeRoy F. Smith and E. B. Jones, Constructive Educational Publishing Co., 111 West Washington Street, Chicago, U. S.

84

virgin birth, blood atonement, bodily resurrection can
well be dispensed with. They may be believed in or dis-
credited individually, and no difference made." '(⁸)

"Sherwood Eddy is at present one of the most menacing
individuals. His well-known liberalism, which amounts
to infidelity, concerning the Scriptures, and his advocacy
of the communism of Russia, render him a fit subject to
join in advocacy of the California anarchistic criminals
whose diabolical endeavors deserved the exact sentence
passed against them. . . . "(⁹)

"In a lecture on Sunday, February 27, 1927, at the
Erlanger Theatre, Chicago, Illinois, Sherwood Eddy outlined his theories regarding Russia. He stated that there
was, of course, a complete denial of liberty and that atheism was rampant, but they had many good things about
their system which completely overshadowed the bad, such
as their system of service for fellowmen and not for private
profit, as no man there was allowed to exploit his fellow-
man; all men are equal regardless of race or color. . . . "(¹⁰)

"During his sojourn in Russia, he again comes to the
front through his laudation of Soviet Russia's government
and policies. At a reception given in Moscow by Mme.
Olga Kameneva, directress of the Bureau of Cultural Relations, Eddy makes the statement: 'Yours is a country
where man no longer exploits man. In its daring ideal it
is the only nation which challenges the world. It challenged the world effectively in China. Many nations
professed friendship for China, but I find that this is the
only nation that has actually made a stand for Chinese
liberty and justice. Your nation stands as a challenge
wherever it plays a role in world affairs.' As a result of
Eddy's pro-Russian attitude and statements, William
Francis, president of the Chicago Y. M. C. A., sent a
protest to Adrian Lyon, Chairman of the Association's
general board and to Fred W. Ramsey of Cleveland,
president of the National Council, demanding that the
statements of Eddy be repudiated, adding that the
Chicago branch disclaimed any connection with them."(¹¹)

(⁸) "The Biblical Recorder," Vol. 17, No. 12.
(⁹) Dr. W. B. Riley in "The Christian Fundamentalist," September 1931.
(¹⁰) "Memorandum" compiled by the American Vigilant Intelli-
gence Federation, November 20, 1931, page 2.
(¹¹) Ibid, page 1.

COMMUNICATION FROM CHANCELLOR ARIE KOK.

'Eddy spoke at DePauw University on February 18,
1931, at a dinner given him by the faculty, after which
he spoke in the Chapel before the students. After an-
nouncing himself an out-and-out socialist, Eddy advocated the adoption of a third party. He gave as his
creed . . . his intention to refuse ever to bear arms
even though he was cast into prison; a full program of
sex education, and laying bare all methods to aid in birth
control, and rediscovery of a religion based on social
justice. After his first talk he offered a number of his
books, which were books on sex, to students. These, he
stated, he was selling at half price. There was a large
sale of them.'([12])
"Eddy resigned from the Y. M. C. A. on January 27,
1931, at a banquet given in his honour on that date, in
New York City at the Commodore Hotel. At the same
time he announced his joining with the Socialist Party
. . . . The "New York Times" of January 28, 1931,
reporting the Eddy banquet, stated: 'In somewhat un-
easy surprise the Y. M. C. A. officials and several important business executives heard Dr. Eddy pledge himself to
fight for economic and political reform, recognition of
Soviet Russia, pacifism, birth control, and revitalization
of religion.'"([13])
"In the July 26 issue of the "Christian Century" appears an article by Eddy on 'What the War Did to My
Mind.' In this article he points out that he has been
liberated first, from the whole war system; second, from
the Old Economic Order; third, from the Old Order of
Conventional Morality. He points out our 'imperialism'
and asserts that man-made laws governing sex morality
are a failure and that Youth must follow its own dictates
unrestrained in the matter of sex. He advocated birth
control to free the American mother from the pagan and
obsolete practice of child birth."([14])
Whatever Dr. Sherwood Eddy may have been a decade
or two ago, it is quite evident that, at present, he is an
outspoken modernist, an advocate of birth control, a
member of the Socialist Party and a Soviet-sympathizer.
This should be clearly understood because of its most

([12]) Ibid, page 8.
([13]) Ibid, page 7, "Chicago Evening American," Dec. 22, 1930.
([14]) Ibid, page 6.

86

COMMUNICATION FROM CHANCELLOR ARIE KOK.

serious implications. There is no possibility of mistaken
judgment, it is a fact, well-established and undeniable.
Those in missionary circles who have their eyes wide open
know all about it and not the least the responsible leaders
in the Y. M. C. A. and in the National Christian Council.
They know the man, his views and his aims better than
anybody else.

And yet, in spite of this all, it was the National Committee of the Y. M. C. A., whose present General Secretary is Dr. David Yü, that invited him for a campaign,
it was the National Christian Council that whole-heartedly
co-operated with him, it was local Churches that opened
their doors for him, it was foreign missionaries who invited
him in their pulpit and it was missionary institutions that
placed their students under his influence. This was done
with a full knowledge of facts, consciously and deliberately.

We further find that at the start of the campaign, "The
Chinese Recorder," a prominent missionary magazine,
edited by the Rev. Frank Rawlinson, said of him: "We
welcome this ardent prophet of a new day!"([15]) and that
"The Bulletin of the National Christian Council," in
which the Rev. C. Lobenstine* and Dr. Cheng Ching Yi
figure prominently, announced his meetings as an "evangelistic campaign."([16]) And when the campaign was in
full swing, it was the same official organ of the N. C. C.
that, in a leading article, eulogized him in the following
words: "Dr. G. Sherwood Eddy—evangelist, writer,
world-traveler and for thirty odd years prophet and
trusted leader among the youth of many nations—is now
in the midst of his eighth visit to China,"([17]) and that,
with evident satisfaction, reported that six of Dr. Eddy's
books (amongst which the "The Challenge of Russia" and
"Sex and Youth") had been translated into Chinese, published by the Y. M. C. A. Press, and were being sold at
considerably less than cost price, "sales having reached as
high as 12,000 volumes sold in a single day."([18])   From

([15]) "The Chinese Recorder," Oct. 1931.
* [A missionary of the Presbyterian Church U. S. A. (J. G. M.).]
([16]) "The Bulletin of the N. C. C.," June 1931, Cf. the article on
      Eddy's meetings in "The China Fundamentalist," July-Sept.
      1931, page 22.
([17]) Ibid, Dec. 14, 1931, page 4.
([18]) Ibid.

COMMUNICATION FROM CHANCELLOR ARIE KOK.

the same Bulletin,(¹⁹) it further appears that a part of
"the gift of gold$10,000, again secured for this fiscal year"
from "our good friend Dr. J. R. Mott" for the purpose of
"the strengthening or the N. C. C. for leadership in the
Five Year Movement"(²⁰) has been used in this Eddy-
campaign.

It is of no use closing one's eyes to these deplorable conditions, neither is it in the best interests of the cause of
Christ in this country, that facts like these are being
hushed up. To feel greatly distressed about this state of
affairs and anxious about the future of the Chinese Church,
as no doubt the majority of the missionaries do, is a hope-
ful sign, but is in itself not sufficient. Merely pitying these
thousands of young men and women who, induced by a
false Christian appeal, run the risk of becoming the vic-
tims of such irresponsible leadership, will not avail, unless
something definitely is done. The fact remains and should
be squarely faced that a heavy responsibility, bordering
on guilt, rests upon the shoulders of those men, who have
either actually sponsored and financed this campaign, or,
passively, tolerated it.

Directly responsible in the first place are the National
Committee of the Y. M. C. A. and the leading men of the
National Christian Council of China, as well as those
Churches and Institutions where Dr. Eddy was invited
to speak. Words are not strong enough to condemn the
attitude of these misguided leaders and we are in hearty
agreement with the editor of the "Biblical Recorder,"
who, quoting "King's Business," says:

"Let our prayers to God be 'reprove Mr. Eddy and all
of his kind; bring them repentant to their knees, or else
hinder them in their soul-destroying work.' "(²¹)

But indirectly, also those particular Mission Boards and
individual supporters at home, that make the activities of
the N. C. C. and kindred organizations possible, must
share the responsibility for this sad state of affairs. It is,
therefore, more imperative than ever that true evangelicals

(¹⁹) Ibid, page 11.
(²⁰) Ibid, page 5.
(²¹) "Biblical Recorder." Vol. 17, No. 12.

COMMUNICATION FROM CHANCELLOR ARIE KOK.

everywhere should refrain from giving to Mission Boards, unless they are fully satisfied as to how their donations are being used on the field.

And, finally, the Missionary Societies and Churches on the field which have associated themselves with the National Christian Council, are likewise implicated as they cannot escape bearing co-responsibility for the actions of a Council of which they are the official members. We can understand the difficult position of loyal elements in the Presbyterian, Methodist, Baptist, and other Missions, which have been drawn into these modernist-controlled bodies by *force majeure* or other causes beyond their control. But there seems to be no particular reason why Missionary Societies as for instance, the "Baseler Mission," which has so many loyal supporters in Switzerland and in Germany, should be in danger of losing their good reputation at home and abroad by being officially affiliated with the N. C. C. If those Missions, which are finding themselves time after time thus placed in an awkward position, had some years ago followed the lead of strong evangelical bodies and declined to join the N. C. C., or had taken the same step the China Inland Mission and its associated societies (Liebenzell Mission, etc.) took, when in 1925 they once for all withdrew from the N. C. C., it is evident that they too would have escaped some very painful experiences, which necessarily result from unholy alliances and tainted relationships.

Two things have again been clearly demonstrated. First, that those Missions and individual Christians, who desire to be loyal to the Christian Faith, the Christian home and Christian civilization cannot remain yoked together with religious bodies which have gradually drifted away from the Truth to such an extent that they do not hesitate to put their imprimatur upon the teachings of a man, who is an avowed modernist, a birth-controller, a Socialist and a Soviet sympathiser. And, second, that the existence on the mission field of such a state of affairs calls for humiliation and penitence on the part of all true believers and at the same time constitutes a new challenge for a united, positive and more effective testimony to the Christ of the Scriptures, the truth of God's Word and the sanctity of Christian life and conduct.

COMMUNICATION FROM CHANCELLOR ARIE KOK.

Hundreds of Presbyterian Churches all over China have been induced to renounce their Presbyterian name and character and to place themselves under the leadership of religious liberals dominating the National Christian Council and the Church of Christ in China. The Board, by cooperating with these bodies and supporting them from mission funds must bear their share in the responsibility that whole sections of the former Presbyterian Constituency in China have been carried away in the maelstrom of modernism.

5. MODERNISM IS PERMITTED TO BE TAUGHT IN PRESBY-TERIAN SCHOOLS.

The modernists' strongholds are the schools. Here they are entrenched and it is here too that children of the Chinese Christians and outsiders are initiated into the first principles of modernism. The results are often most disastrous. Is it not an established fact that the most outspoken anti-christian agitators during the year 1927 were products of mission schools? Speaking, for example, of the "Truth Hall" School of the Northern Presbyterian Mission at Peiping, a senior missionary of the N. P. Board once expressed her great grief and sorrow about conditions there and declared that this School (Principal: the Rev. W. H. Gleysteen)[2] was "a hot-bed of infidelity." It has been in most cases the modernist missionaries who declared themselves in favor of registering mission schools, and it is the conviction of several keen observers that today the Bible would still have its proper place in mission schools, had it not been for the agitation of modernist missionaries and their following amongst the Chinese.

The Board, by supporting modernist educational missionaries and permitting them to propagate modernism in

(2) A missionary of the Presbyterian Church U. S. A. (J. G. M.).

COMMUNICATION FROM CHANCELLOR ARIE KOK.

the mission schools, which were built by and for several decades maintained by mission funds, cannot escape their share in the responsibility for leading the youth astray.

6. FUTURE CHINESE EVANGELISTIC WORKERS ARE BEING SENT FOR THEOLOGICAL TRAINING TO UNION INSTITUTIONS, WITH MODERNISTS ON THEIR TEACHING STAFF.

As an illustration may serve the Union Bible School in the Teng Shih Kou, Peiping, where young women from the Northern Presbyterian Mission are being sent for training in view of future evangelistic work. One lady worker of the Presbyterian Mission is on the teaching staff, giving all her time, but as the school is of the "union" type and the Methodist Mission as well as the American Board Mission (Congregational) are cooperating, it is unescapable, especially in the case of the Congregational teachers, that these future Presbyterian workers are brought under the influence of teachings, which are diametrically opposed to the truth as revealed in the Scriptures and as accepted by true Presbyterians. How far the Congregationalists in Peiping have drifted away from the Truth is apparent from the fact that it was the Congregational Church, which had the sad courage of publishing a booklet, in which Christ was placed on the same level with Lenin and in which Christ's work was explained to be of the same politico-revolutionary character as Lenin's work and Sun Yat Sen's work were.[1]

Is it wise for the Presbyterian Board to cooperate in the theological training of their future evangelists with a Mission like the American Board, which has a right to appoint teachers when it is common knowledge that all of them are theologically unsound and some of them anyhow—as the case may be—are at the same time politically red?

[1] A photostat of the pages of this booklet containing pictures of Lenin, Gandhi, Mazzini, Sun Yat Sen and Jesus will be open to the inspection of Presbytery (J. G. M.).

COMMUNICATION FROM CHANCELLOR ARIE KOK.

7. THE NORTHERN PRESBYTERIAN FOREIGN BOARD CO-
OPERATES WITH AND SUPPORTS INSTITUTIONS OF HIGHER
LEARNING, WHICH ARE VERITIBLE HOTBEDS OF MODERNISM
AND WHICH, IN ONE CASE AT LEAST, WAS AT THE SAME
TIME A CENTER OF COMMUNISM.

This is a most serious indictment and needs unanswerable
evidence. An example of the first is the Cheloo University
at Tsinanfu (Shantung), an example of the second is the
Yenching University of Peiping. Leaving a statement concerning matters obtaining in the Cheloo University to others,
the following observations are made in regard to the affairs
of the Yenching University, Peiping.

a. Modernism in the Yenching University.

The "newer attitude" which the Yenching University had
adopted (modernism pure and simple), was fairly accurately
described by the Editor of the "Peiping Leader" as early
as Nov. 15th, 1922.

Editorial in the "Peking Leader" Wednesday, Nov. 15, 1922.

"CONCERNING YENCHING UNIVERSITY. Fortunately
for those outside as well as those within the organized
Christian bodies the time is rapidly passing when the
principal emphasis in the activities of those organizations
is put on securing adherents to certain creeds. A steadily
increasing number of the leaders inside Christian circles
are taking the position that the important point is not
whether men join the church or verbally express their
faith in certain set of dogmas or even call themselves
by the name of Christ. Rather, they say it is whether
men act on the principles of brotherliness and mutual
helpfulness for which Christ stood. Some are not even
particularly interested in arguing that Christ's statement
of these principles was better than that of other religious
and moral leaders like Buddha, or Socrates or Confucius.
These men call themselves Christian because they see in
Christ's teachings something of unique value, but they

by no means insist that others should see that same
value. They seek rather to persuade others to live
according to the best ideals which each may have, without reference to where those ideals originated. This
newer type of thought inside the Christian circles is not,
of course, popular with the more conservative Christians.
Nevertheless it is only if organized Christianity ceases to
insist on older dogmatic type of faith, if it show itself
willing to simply make the total development of society
whatever contribution it can and at the same time to
welcome the. contribution from all other sources—it is
only if Christianity move in this direction that it will be
able to influence modern social conditions to any great
extent. The day is rapidly passing when any institution
based on any religious or moral theory can maintain an
influence on the lives of men unless it give them complete
freedom to think for themselves and unless it be ready
to revise the credal statements in accordance with the
best thinking outside the organization as well as within.
The day is approaching too, when the only argument as
to the value of a religion or a social theory to which
men will give heed will be the practical one of its effect
on the lives of other men. The time of dogma or dogmatic
faith, that is, is going. This is the reason why when the
Christian missionaries, instead of using their organizations
as a means for securing proselytes to Christianity, have
sought to make only through these organizations the
largest possible contribution to the social welfare and
improvement of the communities in which they are
located, they have secured a steadily increasing influence
outside of the purely Christian circle. In proportion as
they have won for themselves exactly that opportunity
which they seek to make the basic ideas of Christ effective in society, even though they may not have been able
to show any very large number of names on the church
membership rolls. It is because the men and women
now directing the affairs of Yenching University have
taken this newer attitude that this School has come to
be so widely respected entirely outside of merely Christian
circles. These men and women are giving practical expression in their lives to a very real desire to do what they
can to make it more worth while to be alive in China.
They are not much concerned as to whether the students

93

COMMUNICATION FROM CHANCELLOR ARIE KOK.

in the school become professing Christians, rather they
want them to get into their lives the basic principles of
living which they call Christian but which many of them
are perfectly willing to acknowledge also are enunciated
by others.   There are many—not only foreigners but
Chinese; not only in Peking but elsewhere in China—
who do not call themselves Christians and who are opposed
to older type of missionary work who nevertheless are interested in what is being done at Yenching University and
glad to see the work of this school developing along its
present lines.   They feel that the school is making a real
contribution to the development of a higher type of
young men and young women in China and on this basis
their good wishes will go out to the institution in its
present efforts to secure larger financial resources so that
its usefulness may be increased."

Some years later, the dean of the Theological School,
Dr. Timothy T. Lew, gave a description of what the Theological School stood for—modernism pure and simple—
thereby confirming that the Editor of the Peking Leader
was not mistaken.   Dr. T. T. Lew was in those days one
of the Editors of a journal, called "The Truth Weekly,"
a paper most outspoken in radical theological thought.

EXTRACTS FROM A WEEKLY JOURNAL
CALLED "THE TRUTH WEEKLY"

PREPARED FOR THE BIENNIAL CONFERENCE OF THE BIBLE
UNION FOR CHINA, 1926

*Evidence of Modernism in the Chinese Christian
Leaders in Peking, 1-29-26*

The paper was started by seven editors.   Later on Dr.
T. T. Lew and three others joined them, on the Editorial
Board.   These eleven persons are all occupying prominent
positions in Christian institutions and Churches in Peking,
except a few who are independent of Christian support.
Five of them are professors in the Yenching University.
Their names appear in the catalogue of 1925-6 as Pro-
fessors in the Faculty of the School of Religion.   Their

94

COMMUNICATION FROM CHANCELLOR ARIE KOK.

names are the Rev. Dr. T. T. Lew; Rev. Dr. Li Yung-
fang; Jen Yu-wen; Wu Chen-ch'un; and Hsu Pao Ch'ien.
Others are secretaries in the Peking Y. M. C. A. Mr.
Chang Chin Szi, and Hu Hsueh Cheng are among them.
Rev. Pao Kuang-lin is a pastor in a Chinese independent
Church, and member of the N. C. C. Peng Chin Chang
was for some time pastor in the American Board Church,
received a scholarship from the Union Seminary of New
York, where he is now studying.

* * * * * *

Their aim is to investigate the organization and government of the Church, and the reliability of its traditional
doctrines and interpretations. Also to establish the kingdom of heaven on the earth by the reconstruction of society.
Vol. I, No. 1.
The religious tone is definitely modernistic.

* * * * * *

They definitely side with the modernists. Praise Fosdick as one who loves the truth more than he does the
Church. Vol. I, No. 19. They express the hope that the
fundamentalists will not come to China as they hinder
the manifestation of the truth. But they hope that the
modernists will come, and give them help and enlarge
their influence. Vol. I, No. 19.

The BIBLE:—The attitude of the paper regarding the
Bible is consistently destructive. The Bible is written by
ordinary men. The real value only to be discovered by
the critical attitude of the modern scholars. Simply the
record of the development of the religious experience of
the Hebrew people. See Vol. I, No. 6.

* * * * * *

How can we have an unwavering faith in the Bible
when there are evident mistakes in it? How can we fully
obey it when it contains commands which are not suitable
for these days?
The words contained in the Bible can be put on the
same level with the words of foreign and Chinese philoso-
phers of ancient and modern times, as Fosdick, Hu Shih,
Liang Chi-ch'ao, etc. See Vol. I, No. 6.

* * * * * *

COMMUNICATION FROM CHANCELLOR ARIE KOK.

SALVATION:—Their attitude toward SALVATION is antagonistic. *"Break down the superstition of individual salvation, and advocate the social gospel of Jesus."* Vol. I, No. 30.

PRODIGAL SON:—No question of reproof, punishment or ransom . . . .

Why then should we insist on an atonement? If there were really such a doctrine as substitutionary atonement I would myself rather perish, but my conscience would rest in peace. To let one who is innocent and moreover who loves me, be my substitute (if that were needed), what would be the difference to me whether I were to sit at the right hand of God, or to be thrown down to the eighteenth hell? Why do Christians of this generation still try to maintain the doctrine that Jesus, by His blood, made atonement for the sin of the world?

The fact that Jesus did not mention the doctrine of atonement to His disciples proves that He did not want to preach this doctrine, and that He did not want to accomplish this work of atonement . . . Besides this the apostles never emphasized this doctrine; how then, can the doctrine of atonement be the center of Christian teaching? It is simply a matter of tradition. See Vol. I, No. 12. Also No. 10 and No. 11.

* * * * * *

The cause of man's repeatedly falling into sin is selfishness. However Jesus manifested a great love, and practised self denial, and overcame sin. Therefore Christians have only to imitate His self denial in order to be delivered from sin. This kind of salvation is reliable and universal, and there is really nothing mystical about it.

RESURRECTION:—WE cannot but acknowledge the fact of resurrection: but in regard to the question of the way it took place, whether bodily or spiritually, and also as regards the details, it must be stated that this is still a matter of investigation and cannot be decided yet. Vol I, No. 28.

MIRACLES:—There is really nothing miraculous in the casting out of demons . . . .

COMMUNICATION FROM CHANCELLOR ARIE KOK.

The story of the turning of the water into wine, and the money found in the mouth of the fish, do not agree with the principles of Jesus, viz. of not boasting, and of unselfishness. Therefore we can safely put a big question mark beside them. With the progress of science and Biblical research problems like these will be settled in the future. Vol. I, No. 9.

THE VIRGIN BIRTH:—Those in the antichristian movement who despise Jesus because he was a bastard are mistaken, as well as those in the Christian Church who believe in the supernatural conception by the Holy Spirit. Neither Roman soldiers nor God could have been Jesus' Father: He was simply the son of Joseph the carpenter, and Mary, His betrothed wife. . . .

VIEW OF GOD:—The Hebrew view of God gradually developed from polytheism to the Monotheistic consciousness. And their idea of God's character developed from righteousness to holiness, from special love to universal love. Vol. I, No. 6.

Unless our view of God remains the same as that of the people of old (The Hebrews) there is no reason to maintain the doctrine of atonement.

* * * * * *

SOCIAL GOSPEL:—Christ's Gospel is a social Gospel . . . Break down the superstition of individual salvation, and advocate the social gospel of Jesus. Vol. I, No. 30.

Jesus is put in the same category with Dr. Sun Yat Sen, Lenin, Ghandi, and others. Vol. III, No. 23, and fol. numbers.

Jesus is a great revolutionist, and therefore one who follows Jesus must promote revolution. One who is not a revolutionist cannot be counted as a true Christian. . . Most of the Christians do not understand that the idea of the Kingdom of Heaven as preached by Jesus is nothing but the world-revolution. It contains the idea of opposition toward imperialism and capitalism. It suggests freedom for the oppressed nations and practically introduces the idea of communism.

For several years he edited "Life," later combined with "Truth" and called "Truth and Life." It should be re-

COMMUNICATION FROM CHANCELLOR ARIE KOK.

marked here that "Truth and Life" is a recognized publication of the Yenching University as appears from Mrs. Sharman's statement on page 10 of her booklet "Yenching University, an Interpretation," corroborated by Dr. J. L. Stuart's Introduction to this booklet.

> "Members of Yenching's School of Religion have from the beginning carried a large share of the editorial work for the progressive journal called *Truth and Life.*" (Mrs. H. B. Sharman; *Yenching University, an Interpretation,* p. 10.)

Special attention is drawn to Vol. VI, No. 5 of March 1, 1932, where Andrew C. Y. Cheng, Professor of Theology at the Yenching University, plainly denies the deity of Christ,

> "One of the most tragic blunders of Christianity has been the placing of such extreme emphasis upon the uniqueness of Jesus that a great difference has been created between him and the rest of mankind. If all human beings are created in the spiritual image of God and if there is only one kind of personality, then the only difference between Jesus and ourselves is one of maturity. Of course that difference is a tremendous one, for he climbed far higher than the rest of us have ever been able to reach. But his very purpose in living was to enable his followers to live as he lived and if need be to die as he died." (Andrew C. Y. Cheng: "Following Jesus," in *Truth and Life*, Vol. VI, No. 5, March 1, 1932, p. 2.)

without any protest on the part of the six North Presbyterian missionaries, whose names appear on the inside of the title page, nor of the President of the University, Dr. J. Leighton Stuart, a Southern Presbyterian Missionary, whose name is also mentioned amongst the others. In another statement, Jesus is declared fallible and His deity is again denied in unmistakable terms.

COMMUNICATION FROM CHANCELLOR ARIE KOK.

"I do desire to point out, however, that Jesus was by no means infallible, and that in some of our ethical and religious thought we have gone beyond him. Moreover, in making him our God, instead of one of the great human leaders of the race, we have robbed him of much of his vitality, and have done violence in all probability to his own conception of his person and work. As long as we missionaries believe that in Jesus, or in the Christian experience, we have something that is uniquely final in the sense that it is directly God-given, I believe that we will be shut out from the most rewarding fellowship with non-Christian Chinese. No matter how liberal and tolerant we may be if, we are confident we have the Truth, there is bound to be latent in our attitude a certain dogmatism which will wall us away from people who do not see things as we do."

(Quoted from "an article that came out in the magazine issued by the [Yenching] University and written by one of the professors" by M. A. Hopkins in *The China Fundamentalist*, Vol. V, No. 2, October-December, 1932, p. 33).

An article, written by the present dean of the School of Religion, T. C. Chao in the "Chinese Recorder" of November, 1930, shows that the latter closely follows in the steps of his predecessor, T. T. Lew.

FROM "THE CHINESE RECORDER,"
NOVEMBER 1930

ARTICLE BY T. C. CHAO, *Dean of the School of Religion of the Yenching University, Peiping.*

Page 684:

". . . On the side of the Church there are many missionaries who have returned to their homeland never to come back. Some intelligent, progressive missionaries, able to cooperate with the Chinese Christians, have taken a position of modesty and retreat, thus gradually dropping out of sight. But unintelligent reactionary fundamentalists, who claim that they were not sent by man, continue to come in increasing numbers. . . ."

COMMUNICATION FROM CHANCELLOR ARIE KOK.

Page 685:

". . . In spite of this Christianity in China still has three weaknesses. The first is internal strife—the conservative and modern points of view in faith occupy almost irreconcilable positions. The modern side desires to find harmony with modern science and philosophy on the one hand and to make definite connections with modern social living conditions on the other hand, hoping to make religion and life one. Its object, therefore, is to receive, to be tolerant, to fill the entire life with religion. The conservative party has taken up an absolutely intolerant position. Apart from detailed differences in faith and creeds, the numerous communions in the Christian Church also differ in organization, policies, work and activities. Therefore the Christian community although numbering over 300,000, does not (perhaps cannot) unite and work together for the exemplification of the spirit of Christ and the effective upholding of his teachings. . . ."

The plain and undeniable fact is, that the Yenching University has been steadily drifting away towards the extreme left of theological thought, a point where it stands to-day.

b. Communism in the Yenching University.

In the years 1926 and 1927 it was known in Peiping that the Yenching University harboured teachers, who were in full sympathy with the Soviet Revolution and who advocated Soviet ideas amongst the students. Propaganda was carried on in an underhand way until, in December, 1927, they came out in the open by publishing a monthly paper, called "The China Outlook." The names of the editors appeared on the first page: Maxwell S. Stewart, T. Arthur Bisson (both on the staff of the Yenching University) Lucius Porter (Dean of the Arts School of the same institution) and Stuart Allen (a Y. M. C. A. worker).
* * * The paper was printed at the "Peking Leader

COMMUNICATION FROM CHANCELLOR ARIE KOK.

Press," a printing establishment in the city of Peking. On the inside of the cover it is stated that "Communication should be addressed to Maxwell S. Stewart, Chengfu, Peking, China." Chengfu is simply the site of the Yenching University. The Editors were actually living on the grounds of the Yenching University, where the paper was both edited and issued. Only the printing was done outside.

After the publication of the first issue, which was "red" enough to forbode trouble, the Peking Leader Press deemed it prudent to suppress their name as printer and the three other editors withheld their names too, so that only Stewart's name and address at Yenching University were left for editorial communications. The others continued, however, their work as contributing editors, and, in spite of everything, the paper was permitted by the authorities of the Yenching University to be issued for at least eight months.

On November 20th, 1928, the paper was re-named "China Tomorrow," the Yenching address was replaced by "P. O. Box No. 8" and the name of Stewart disappeared too, some Chinese names figuring as an Editorial Board. The whole thing was, in fact, a camouflage and—although less outspoken than in "The China Outlook"—the pro-Russian propaganda, centering in the Yenching University, was continued as before, both through the paper in its new garb and through cell-activities.

As for the contents of these journals reference is made to a book review written by Mr. A. Kok in the "China Fundamentalist," Vol. II, No. 1, page 37, where all necessary details are given.

CHINA TOMORROW. *Editors:* YEN CHING YUEH, BIEN SHA KING, WU JUI KAO, FANG FU AN. *P. O. Box No. 8, Peiping, China. $2.– per year, Foreign U. S. $1.50.*

There would seem to be no special reason for introducing to our readers a periodical, which bears on its title page

101

COMMUNICATION FROM CHANCELLOR ARIE KOK.

four, five or six names in Chinese (Romanized) of unknown
persons, who constitute its editorial board, and which gives
no information whatever as to the editorial connections,
neither in any way indicates, where the paper is being
issued, published or printed, beyond a Post Box address.

Usually papers of such an obscure origin are looked upon
with suspicion and are laid aside, even if, as in this case,
the front page informs the reader that he has to do
with "the periodical of New China, dedicated to the
masses. . . ."

But the matter becomes somewhat different, when the
casual reader of a report, entitled: "Yen Ching University,
an Interpretation," by Mrs. H. B. Sharman, a member of
the Staff, discovers that the periodical under review is referred to in these words: "Some of our staff are interested
in the newly launched journal of public opinion called
'China Tomorrow'" (p. 10).

In the above report only four periodicals are named and
if "China Tomorrow" is considered important enough to
be classified in the same category with the others as being
a means "through which the light that shines at Yenching
radiates," then it is well worth knowing what kind of light
it is, that is being spread by this periodical of 16 large-
sized pages in English, when each month of the year, it
enters into the various Christian Colleges and Universities.

It should be noted here that the Yenching University is
a Union Missionary Institution, largely supported by
funds obtained from Presbyterian, Methodist and Congregational Missions and donors in America and England,
the students "paying less than 12% of the cost of their
education" (p. 11).

It is impossible to get a good idea of what "China Tomorrow" really is, without knowing its progenitor and
immediate predecessor, called "The China Outlook."
The latter is the former under a new name but the spirit
moving behind both papers is the same. It is one paper
adapted to different times and occasions.

What, then, is "The China Outlook"?

There was nothing obscure about its first number. The
paper was introduced as a "liberal and constructive journal of opinion," edited by American missionaries. The
names of the editors, Maxwell S. Stewart, T. Arthur Bisson
(Yenching professors) and of the contributing editors

COMMUNICATION FROM CHANCELLOR ARIE KOK.

Stuart Allen (of the Y. M. C. A.), Lucius Porter (Yenching professor) appeared on the first page. Communications to be addressed to Maxwell S. Stewart, Chengfu (viz., Yenching University), Peking, China. Printed at the Peking Leader Press.

It will be remembered that at the time, when the first issue of this paper appeared, December, 1927, Communism was on the decline in China. Radical movements in North-China had been suppressed. Free speech was not permitted and the least manifestation on the part of the Chinese of sympathy with the Russian cause, might have fatal results. Owing to their different status, foreigners were, of course, in a quite different position.

The first editorial opened by stating: "At the present time it is impossible for such a journal to be issued under Chinese auspices without grave risk to the editors, so the present editors have taken upon themselves the task of reflecting progressive Chinese public opinion as they see it." And somewhat further on: "More and more it is becoming apparent that there is only one salvation for China—a genuine social revolution along the lines outlined by Madame Sun Yat-sen. Until the time is ripe for that revolution the shiftings and bickerings of the present school of militarists will be as meaningless as a national election in the United States of America."

T. A. Bisson wrote an article on "Russia's Tenth Anniversary," in which he comes to this conclusion: "The Soviet Union, Persia, Afghanistan, Turkey, and China have a common interest in checkmating the great Western imperialist powers . . . . The U. S. S. R. is waging a campaign for the economic and political consolidation of Eurasia. The constituent states have a common ambition for the realization of a system of society that will eliminate exploitation and make the self-determination of peoples a reality. The Soviet Union has presented a simple principle of action to the Asiatic peoples: Cooperate and be free."

The first number also contains an article by Earl Browder, entitled "The Chinese Peasant Movement." The character of its contents may be surmised, when one remembers that Earl Browder is a former member of the I. W. W. and is described in the police reports as "one of the chief agents of the Comintern, who are now centering their efforts on Communist cells in the rural districts of

COMMUNICATION FROM CHANCELLOR ARIE KOK.

China attempting to form a sort of proletarian-peasant league which will cooperate in an effort to sovietize China." (U. P. October 1928). He is also active in matters of the Pan-Pacific Trade Union. At its last annual confab "which was held in Shanghai in the strictest secrecy, Russia and America were represented by only one delegate each. Earl Browder, of the Trade Union Educational League of America, presided over the meeting. The report declared that the hold of the Third International on the Shanghai Labour Unions had not been broken. Though thousands of individuals have been destroyed, most of our "cells" (nuclei) survive . . . . (Weekly Review December 1928).

Miss Grace M. Boyton contributed a lengthy article on "The Eastern Tide in Western Affairs" and Maxwell S. Stewart deals with the question "Can Capitalism solve China's problems"? He concluded: "The fact remains that the retention of the capitalist system is a far greater menace to the future of China than any of the other evils which threaten the nation."

Finally, T. A. Bisson wrote a sympathetic review of "Communism" by Laski, who sees in Lenin "one of the supreme political strategists of modern history" and "the ideal leader for the situation" in the Russia of 1917.

The whole trend of the first number was such as to arouse grave suspicions in responsible quarters that the Communistic Party had succeeded in forming a "cell" even in one of the leading liberal missionary institutions of China.

The second number showed both marks of apprehension and of prudence. The names of the editors had disappeared and the printers too had deemed it advisable to drop their name from the paper. Otherwise, no change was noticeable. With undaunted courage, worthy of a better cause, the editors continued to issue the paper at regular times. Maxwell S. Stewart and T. H. Bisson did most of the editing. Miss Grace M. Boyton, Leonard S. Hsü (both on the Yenching Staff), Stuart Allen (of the Y. M. C. A.), Dr. Harry F. Ward (ref. The China Fundamentalist No. 4, p. 45), Earl Browder (Bolshevik Agent), Frank Rawlinson (Editor of the "Chinese Recorder") contributed articles.

Space forbids to give a detailed summary of the con-

COMMUNICATION FROM CHANCELLOR ARIE KOK.

tents of the paper, but this is sure that a careful study of
it will convince any unprejudiced reader that the majority
of the editorials, articles and reviews were written or
reprinted with the set purpose to advance the Russian
cause in China, to arouse students, labourers and peasants
to direct revolutionary action and to propagate "liberal"
ideas in regard to birth control, etc.

Titles like these speak volumes: "The Economic Re-
habilitation of Soviet Russia" (No. 2), "Missionaries,
Communists, and Mutual Tolerance" (No. 3), "Peace
out of Russia" (No. 3), "What is Russia's Future?"
(No. 4), "Manifesto of the Pan-Pacific Trade Union
Secretariat" (No. 4), "The Imperialist Dilemma in China"
(No. 5), "Report of the All-China Labour Federation"
(No. 5), "Birth Control for China" (No. 6), "Declaration
of the Soviet Delegation at Geneva, Litvinov's Speech"
(No. 6), etc.

During the summer of 1928, when Communisn had
become extremely unpopular in China, "The China Outlook" suddenly failed to appear, but in November it
re-appeared under a new name, "China Tomorrow," under
a new editorial board of four Chinese editors and with a
new address, P. O. Box 8.

Superficially, "China Tomorrow" makes the appearance
of an altogether new paper, but the careful observer does
not fail to notice that it is being printed at the same Press
and edited at the same University as before. And although
the foreign editors have taken the background, the pen
of the foreign missionary is still extremely active. A
more restrained policy has been adopted, but the principles and the object have remained the same.

This is evident from editorials, articles and reviews,
covering subjects like: "Birth Control in China" (No. 1),
"The Chinese Peasant Movement" (No. 2), "Marx and
Lenin" (No. 2), "Have we betrayed Sun Yat Sen?"
(No. 3), "The Chinese Trade Union Movement in 1928"
(No. 4), "The Need of Family Limitation" (No. 4), "New
Schools in New Russia" (No. 4), "Impressions of Soviet
Russia" (No. 4), "The Diary of a Communist School-
boy" (No. 4), "Lenin" (No. 5), etc.

The sympathy of the editors is with the "left-wingers"
and no attempt is made to hide their hope and expectation
that eventually, the "radicals" will succeed and come to
power (pp. 70–72, 87, 90, 93, etc.).

COMMUNICATION FROM CHANCELLOR ARIE KOK.

We must conclude this survey with the following observations.

It is evident that "China Tomorrow" is a paper with outspoken pro-Russian sympathies, aiming at the spread of Soviet revolutionary ideas amongst the students of Christian and other Institutions. Its religious tone is modernistic and highly destructive.

It is very regrettable that such a paper is issued from an institution, that claims to be Christian and obtains support from mission-funds.

It is a matter of great surprise that such a paper is characterized by a member of the staff as being typical of "the light that shines at Yenching" and that the President of this University, a Presbyterian missionary, endorses this report, including the reference to "China Tomorrow," by stating in his Foreword, that this report is a recast of "the annual reports of the university's executive officers." (We presume our Book Editor must refer to Rev. J. L. Stuart, D.D., but in a personal letter he expressed strong disapproval of Bolshevism.—Ed.)

We consider it our duty to draw the serious attention of the authorities of our evangelical colleges and schools and of our evangelical church-leaders in China to this publication, which is being sent all over the country, and to sound a note of warning in view of its pernicious influence on young and inexperienced Christians.

The light that shines through this paper is not borrowed from the Word of God, which has been given to us as a light unto our path. It is a false light, a wandering light, that leads away from Christ into ways of lawlessness, unbelief, sin, and destruction.

K.

Even a casual perusal of these papers will clearly show the pro-Soviet attitude of the Editors.

After having thus carried on with his comrades his communistic propaganda as a missionary on the staff of the Yenching University, Maxwell Stewart left for Moscow, where he became editor of an English language newspaper, called "The Moscow News." A photostat of this paper proves beyond doubt the fact of his editorship of a Soviet

COMMUNICATION FROM CHANCELLOR ARIE KOK.

paper in Moscow. His re-appearance in Moscow explains his activities in the Yenching University and throws a sharp light on the attitude of the authorities of this University, permitting a man of his type to use the University as a base for subversive propaganda for more than three years.

Another example of red propaganda carried out by a group of men, of which several are on the staff of the Yenching University, is the publication in Chinese some years ago of the "Truth Seeking Series." For details reference is made to a book review written by Mr. A. Kok for the China Fundamentalist, Vol. I, No. 4, May 1929.

> TRUTH SEEKING SERIES. *Published (in Chinese) by the Publication Committee of North China Kung Li Huei (American Board), Teng Shih Kow, Peking.*
>
> No. 6. FIVE GREAT LEADERS OF THE PEOPLE. *By* NEANDER C. S. CHANG. *83 pages. (Titles and names are taken from an announcement in English.)*

This series contains ten booklets, composed or translated by the Rev. Timothy T. Lew (No. 1), the Rev. Li Jung Fang (Nos. 4, 5), Wu Lai Chuan, (Nos. 2, 3), all professors of the Yen Ching University at Peiping, a Union Missionary Institution, the Rev. K. L. Pao (Nos. 7, 8), member of the Editorial Board of the "Chinese Recorder" Shanghai, member of the National Christian Council and Secretary of the Y. M. C. A., and Neander C. S. Chang (Nos. 6, 9, 10), Secretary of the Y. M. C. A., and, for some time, lecturer at the North China Language School of Peiping.

No. 6 of this series deals with five great men, who in the eyes of the author, have distinguished themselves because of "their brave struggle for the people." These heroes are: Lenin, Gandhi, Mazzini, Sun Yat-sen and Jesus. Pictures of each of them serve as illustrations.

Two of them are of special interest, viz. Lenin and Jesus.

The chapter on Lenin commences with a description of his native place, youth, parents, family relations, home,

COMMUNICATION FROM CHANCELLOR ARIE KOK.

his exemplary character, his love for study and his compassion for the people, who greatly suffered under the yoke of the Tsarist rule. Then, it is related, how he resolved to become a saviour of the masses and joined the revolutionary party, how he was imprisoned, was forced to flee for his life, suffered many hardships and how, in spite of several futile attempts to start the revolution, he never thought of giving up the struggle, but courageously fought to the end. He is honoured as the most successful follower of Marx (p. 11), as a man of exceptional simplicity, of great devotion and love for the masses. His sole aim in life was to strive for the people, to liberate the oppressed, to build up a communistic world, in which the principles of communism could be realised. Unfortunately, as a result of the consequences of an attempt on his life, he died. But he died for others, his object was accomplished, the revolution had succeeded. "From the beginning to the end throughout his whole life he fought and sacrificed himself for the oppressed people of the world" (p. 14).

There is a class of people, who, whilst wilfully ignoring terror, outrage, crime, sin, murder and everything else that is Satanic, love to pay homage to Lenin and eulogize him as a saviour of the masses. But such people are invariably self-confessed bolsheviks. Of Y. M. C. A. secretaries and teachers of missionary institutions, something different might be expected.

Chapter V, entitled "Jesus" commences with the statement, that although the principles and methods of these five leaders are different, yet, the object for which each of them fought in life was, in every case, the same, namely: liberating oppressed people. The life of Jesus proves, says the author, that he too had no other aim (p. 65). Therefore, on the very first day when he entered upon his lifework, Jesus said to the people: "The Spirit of the Lord is upon me . . . he has sent me to preach deliverance to the captives . . . to set at liberty them that are bruised." (p. 66).

After this introduction, Jesus is pictured as a revolutionary leader. As in the case of Lenin his youth, parents, family-relations, home, his exemplary character, his wisdom and compassion for the oppressed people are discussed in detail. Then it is related how Jesus resolved to become the Messiah, a Saviour to his people; how he,

108

COMMUNICATION FROM CHANCELLOR ARIE KOK.

being doubtless influenced by his fellow-provincial Judas, likewise a revolutionary leader, made up his mind to deliver the Jews from under the oppressing yoke of Imperialist Rome. And how, later on, he desired to extend his saving power to all oppressed people of the world. Jesus is further pictured as a man of great simplicity, of remarkable power and showing exceptional love to the people. He was opposed to the use of force; he preached love, sacrifice and obedience to God. At the same time he did the utmost to free the people from the shackles of the Jewish religion.

However, the opposition party at Jerusalem become aware of his plans. He was repeatedly forced to flee to Galilee and to change his attitude, but like Lenin, he was not discouraged by early failures, but fought courageously to the very end. Finally Judas, being disappointed because of Jesus' hesitation to start the revolution, joined the opposition party at Jerusalem. This party, together with the religious rulers of that time, arrested Jesus, declared him guilty of sedition and crucified him. Strange enough, he is described as having appeared to his disciples after his death.

This serious but futile attempt to make of Jesus a revolutionary leader, of the Lenin-type, is not merely a clever piece of red propaganda, it is an outrage against Scripture, history, truth, conscience and common sense, and most repulsive to the sacred feelings of all Christian people. It is dragging Jesus Christ, the Son of the Living God from His throne, robbing Him of His crown, bringing Him down to the level of common men and degrading Him to a class of political agitators. It is denying the Holy One and the Just, crucifying the Son of God afresh and desiring Barabbas, who, like Lenin, was a murderer, in His stead.

* * * * * *

As "Five Great Leaders of the People," in which Christ was placed on the same level with Lenin and the work of Jesus was represented to be of the same politico-revolutionary character as that of Lenin, is out of print, an interesting photostat of the most important pages with illustrations is attached hereto.[1]

(1) See footnote under Section 6 above.

COMMUNICATION FROM CHANCELLOR ARIE KOK.

As since 1929 all communistic propaganda and activities in China are mercilessly suppressed by the Chinese authorities, open pro-Soviet propaganda is now impossible, but there is ample reason to believe that the fire is still smoldering at Yenching University, only awaiting a favorable time to flame up again in new vigor. Mr. Stewart and Mr. Bisson have gone, but Mr. Ritter, who was one of their group, is still teaching in Yenching and several Chinese professors of pro-Soviet tendencies are being maintained on the staff. They are, as the future will show, biding their time.

    c. Northern Presbyterian Missionaries involved.

Special mention should be made here of the fact that of the three missionaries, who were most actively engaged in the publication of "The China Outlook" and "China Tomorrow," two are officially catalogued as Northern Presbyterian Missionaries, viz., A. T. Bisson* and R. H. Ritter. This means that Northern Presbyterian Mission funds have been used to support Northern Presbyterian missionaries, who, instead of preaching the Gospel, were actually carrying on pro-Soviet propaganda on the mission-field.

    d. The Board's responsibility.

The latest Directory of Protestant Missions shows that in 1932 ten Northern Presbyterian Missionaries were on the staff of the Yenching University. They are catalogued as missionaries under the North China Mission of the Northern Presbyterians. Their salaries are paid from mission funds, granted by the Board. The next annual missionary meeting of the whole of the North China Mission

* Not listed as a missionary in Report of the Board of Foreign Missions of the Presbyterian Church U. S. A. for 1932. (J. G. M.)

of the Northern Presbyterian Mission, will take place in the Yenching University. It was stated by a missionary under the Northern Presbyterian Board in a most positive way, that cooperation with the Yenching University costs the Board a sum of gold$25,000 annually. There are no means of finding out at this time whether the amount is still as high as that. But the exact figure is not of first importance: it is the principle involved.

The fact remains, that the Board for more than ten years, has cooperated with an institution which is rankly modernist in character and which tolerates pro-Soviet teachers on the staff and continues to cooperate until this day in spite of everything that has happened.

Is the Board, as a steward of mission funds, justified in continuing giving support to an institution, that leads the youth into modernism and communism? Can the Board escape her share in the responsibility for the awful consequences of this cooperation for the Christian Church?

The Northern Presbyterian Foreign Board would be well advised

1. to reconsider their stand on the "inclusive policy" on the field;

2. to free the missions from all unholy alliances and entanglements with modernistic bodies and groups;

3. to see to it that mission funds are not misappropriated but are used exclusively for Christian mission work in the biblical sense;

4. to repudiate modernism on the mission field and promote, as before, exclusively, the preaching by their missionaries of the only true Gospel of Jesus Christ, as revealed in the Holy Scriptures, and as accepted by historic Presbyterianism.

PRESS OF
ALLEN, LANE & SCOTT
PHILADELPHIA

TITLES IN THIS SERIES

The Evangelical Matrix
1875-1900

■ 10. Arthur T. Pierson, ed.
*The Inspired Word: A Series of Papers and
Addresses Delivered at the Bible Inspiration Conference,
Philadelphia, 1887*
London, 1888

■ 11. Moody Bible Institute Correspondence
Dept. *First Course — Bible Doctrines, Instructor—
R. A. Torrey; Eight Sections with Questions,*
Chicago, 1901

The Formation of
A Fundamentalist Agenda
1900-1920

■ 12. Amzi C. Dixon,
Evangelism Old and New,
New York, 1905

■ 13. William Bell Riley
*The Finality of the Higher Criticism;
or, The Theory of Evolution and False Theology*
Minneapolis, 1909

■ 14.-17 George M. Marsden, ed.
The Fundamentals: A Testimony to the Truth
New York, 1988

■ 18. Joel A. Carpenter, ed.
The Bible in Faith and Life,
as Taught by James M. Gray
New York, 1988

■ 19. Mark A. Noll, ed.
The Princeton Defense
of Plenary Verbal Inspiration
New York, 1988

■ 20. *The Victorious Life:*
Messages from the Summer Conferences
Philadelphia, 1918

■ 21. Joel A. Carpenter, ed.
Conservative Call to Arms
New York, 1988

■ 22. *God Hath Spoken: Twenty-five Addresses*
Delivered at the World Conference on
Christian Fundamentals, May 25- June 1, 1919
Philadelphia, 1919

Fundamentalism Versus Modernism
1920-1935

■ 23. Joel A. Carpenter, ed.
The Fundamentalist -Modernist Conflict:
Opposing Views on Three Major Issues
New York, 1988

■ 24. Joel A. Carpentar, ed.
Modernism and Foreign Missions:
Two Fundamentalist Protests
New York, 1988

■ 25. John Horsch
Modern Religious Liberalism: The Destructiveness
and Irrationality of Modernist Theology
Scottsdale, Pa., 1921

■ 26. Joel A. Carpenter,ed.
Fundamentalist vesus Modernist
The Debates Between
John Roach Stratton and Charles Francis Potter
New York, 1988

■ 27. Joel A. Carpenter, ed.
William Jennings Bryan on
Orthodoxy, Modernism, and Evolution
New York, 1988

■ 28. Edwin H. Rian
The Presbyterian Conflict
Grand Rapids, 1940

Sectarian Fundamentalism
1930-1950

■ 29. Arno C. Gaebelein
Half a Century: The Autobiography of a Servant
New York, 1930

■ 30. Charles G. Trumball
Prophecy's Light on Today
New York, 1937

■ 31. Joel A. Carpenter, ed.
Biblical Prophecy in an Apocalyptic Age:
Selected Writings of Louis S. Bauman
New York, 1988

■ 32. Joel A. Carpenter, ed.
Fighting Fundamentalism:
Polemical Thrusts of the 1930s and 1940s
New York, 1988

■ 33. *Inside History of First Baptist Church, Fort*
Worth, and Temple Baptist Church, Detroit:
Life Story of Dr. J. Frank Norris
Fort Worth, 1938

■ 34. John R. Rice
The Home — Courtship, Marriage, and Children: A
Biblical Manual of Twenty -Two Chapters
on the Christian Home.
Wheaton, 1945

■ 35. Joel A. Carpenter, ed.
Good Books and the Good Book: Reading Lists by
Wilbur M. Smith, Fundamentalist Bibliophile
New York, 1988

■ 36. H. A. Ironside
Random Reminiscences from Fifty Years of Ministry
New York, 1939

■ 37 Joel A. Carpenter,ed.
*Sacrificial Lives: Young Martyrs
and Fundamentalist Idealism*
New York, 1988.

Rebuilding, Regrouping, & Revival
1930-1950

■ 38. J. Elwin Wright
*The Old Fashioned Revival Hour
and the Broadcasters*
Boston, 1940

■ 39. Joel A. Carpenter, ed.
*Enterprising Fundamentalism:
Two Second-Generation Leaders*
New York, 1988

■ 40. Joel A. Carpenter, ed.
Missionary Innovation and Expansion
New York, 1988

■ 41. Joel A. Carpenter, ed.
*A New Evangelical Coalition: Early Documents
of the National Association of Evangelicals*
New York, 1988

■ 42. Carl McIntire
Twentieth Century Reformation
Collingswood, N. J., 1944

■ 43. Joel A. Carpenter, ed.
The Youth for Christ Movement and Its Pioneers
New York, 1988

■ 44. Joel A. Carpenter, ed.
The Early Billy Graham:
Sermons and Revival Accounts
New York, 1988

■ 45. Joel A. Carpenter, ed.
Two Reformers of Fundamentalism:
Harold John Ockenga and Carl F. H. Henry
New York, 1988

DATE DUE

GAYLORD			PRINTED IN U.S.A.